STUDIES IN FRENCH LITERATURE No. 21

General Editor

W. G. Moore
Fellow and Tutor of St. John's College, Oxford

PRÉVOST:

MANON LESCAUT

by
VIVIENNE MYLNE
Senior Lecturer in French
University of Kent at Canterbury

EDWARD ARNOLD

© VIVIENNE MYLNE 1972

First published 1972
by Edward Arnold (Publishers) Ltd.
25 Hill Street, London W1X 8LL

PQ
2021
.M33M9
C.1

Cloth edition ISBN: 0 7131 5644 9
Paper edition ISBN: 0 7131 5645 7

Printed in Great Britain by
The Camelot Press Ltd., London and Southampton

Contents

1. THE AUTHOR AND THE BACKGROUND   7

2. THE MAN OF QUALITY: FIRST NARRATOR AND MORALIST   14

3. MANON: THE ENIGMATIC HEROINE   21

4. DES GRIEUX: NARRATOR AND 'ÂME SENSIBLE'   29

5. LESCAUT: REALISM AND VERISIMILITUDE   40

6. MANON'S 'PROTECTORS': THE ROLE OF MONEY   48

7. DES GRIEUX PÈRE AND TIBERGE: TWO MORAL CODES   53

8. THE NEW WORLD: THE DÉNOUEMENT AND THE MORAL   60

    BIBLIOGRAPHICAL NOTE   64

Acknowledgements

This study of *Manon Lescaut* is deeply indebted to the work of Frédéric Deloffre and Raymond Picard, and in particular to the Introduction to their critical edition of this novel. The Publishers are grateful to Messrs. Garnier for permission to reproduce copyright material from this edition.

My thanks are also due to my colleague, Philip Robinson, who read this study in typescript and provided helpful comments and suggestions.

1. The Author and the Background

Antoine-François Prévost was born on April 1st, 1697, at Hesdin. His best-known work, *Manon Lescaut*, was published in Holland in 1731. Do the events of Prévost's life up to 1731 provide us with any clues for a better understanding of the novel?

Manon is the story of a love-affair: a young man, the Chevalier des Grieux, suffers all the problems and indignities of falling passionately in love with a girl whom most people consider to be unsuitable for him. Throughout most of the story Manon is gay, thoughtless, pleasure-loving. Her desire for pleasure makes her willing to leave Des Grieux when he runs short of money, and turn to richer men who can pay for her amusements. It is this trait which shapes the plot. After an initial brief spell of happiness when they have run away together, the lovers part because Manon accepts the attentions of a rich financier. Separated from Manon, the Chevalier comes to believe that his feeling for her is dead, but a single meeting revives his passion, and he again runs away with her. From this point onwards, disasters and misdeeds accumulate: the couple twice lose their money, by fire and theft; the Chevalier takes to cardsharping as a source of income. On two more occasions Manon plans to leave the Chevalier for a richer man, but is won back by Des Grieux's pleading and agrees to trick her new 'protector'. These incidents lead to Manon being first imprisoned and then sentenced to deportation. The Chevalier accompanies her to America, and there it seems as though they have at last found happiness. However, disaster overtakes them again, and Manon dies when they are attempting to escape from the colony.

Many biographers and critics have maintained that the characters and situations in *Manon* were based on Prévost's own experience, so that the book is, in the main, autobiographical. During the last fifty years or so, however, painstaking researches have revealed that there is no reliable evidence to support this suggestion.

Frédéric Deloffre, in the edition of *Manon Lescaut* which he prepared with Raymond Picard,[1] sets out in detail the factual information that

[1] Paris, Garnier, 1965. In this study, all page-numbers for quotations from *Manon* refer to this edition.

has so far been traced concerning these years of Prévost's life. There are still some gaps and uncertainties; it seems, for instance, that Prévost twice entered military service, but scarcely anything is known about these episodes. Before the second of these periods with the army, Prévost had undergone part of the training required for becoming a Jesuit priest. But in 1720, when it seemed that he had at last decided on his true calling, he settled down to become not a Jesuit but a Benedictine, taking his vows as a member of the community known as the Congrégation de Saint-Maur.

By 1728, when he was at the monastery of Saint-Germain-des-Prés in Paris, Prévost had come to feel that his choice was the wrong one. He asked for, and was granted, permission to transfer into another branch of the Benedictine order, in which he could enjoy more freedom. But because he left Saint-Germain before the permission to do so had been officially promulgated, he put himself on the wrong side of the law. He fled to England, where he stayed for about two years and obtained a post as tutor to the son of Sir John Eyles. Prévost then, it seems, paid court to Sir John's daughter Mary, who accepted, in secret, his proposal of marriage. But the affair came to light; Prévost, predictably, lost his job, and late in 1730 he left England for Holland. Here, until mid-1731, he apparently spent most of his time writing. The same few months saw the printing and publication of the final three volumes of the *Mémoires et aventures d'un Homme de Qualité*. (The first four volumes, written while Prévost was still a Benedictine, had been published in 1728 and 1729.) The seventh and last volume is of course the story now generally referred to as *Manon Lescaut*. All three volumes were on sale in Holland by the end of May, 1731.

It was not, however, until 1733 that an edition of *Manon* appeared in France. This led some critics, ignorant or sceptical of information about the earlier Amsterdam editions, to decide that the true date of publication was 1733. It was precisely this 'fact' which made possible the argument that *Manon Lescaut* was largely autobiographical. For towards the middle of 1731, Prévost made the acquaintance of Lenki Eckhardt, who was (as far as we know) the one great love of his life. She was a woman of extravagant tastes who had already, according to contemporary comments, ruined several lovers. Prévost in his turn found that he could not make enough money to satisfy her demands, and ran disastrously into debt.

The parallel with Manon, and her need for money and pleasure, is all

THE AUTHOR AND THE BACKGROUND 9

too obvious. But as *Manon Lescaut* had already been published by the time Prévost was embarking upon his liaison with Lenki, we cannot interpret the book as an account of his recent sufferings. Moreover it seems misguided to assume, as do some partisans of the autobiographical view, that the book would be in some way more interesting or 'better' for being based largely upon the author's personal memories. The element of fidelity to the writer's own experience is quite irrelevant when it comes to judging the artistic merits of a narrative.

The Lenki episode can still be used as evidence, but for a different purpose. It reveals that Prévost himself was the kind of man who could fall victim to an overwhelming love for a woman whom other people considered to be unworthy of him. There are further similarities of character and temperament between Prévost and Des Grieux: for instance, both could appreciate, for a time at least, the attractions of a life of peaceful study; both showed a tendency to explain away their discreditable actions rather than accept blame for them. From such parallels one may conclude that Des Grieux encompasses certain traits of Prévost's own character. But it would be rash to assume either that Des Grieux is in any sense a complete portrait of Prévost, or even that Prévost was consciously aware how much of himself he was contributing to the creation of Des Grieux.

If then we are looking for background knowledge which will inform our reading of *Manon Lescaut*, we shall find it not so much in Prévost's individual life-history as in the social history of his day and in the literary history of the development of fiction in France.

From the history of social institutions we can learn, for instance, that Des Grieux's father did not exceed the limits of parental authority accepted at the time; repressive as he may seem to some modern readers, he did not even act as sternly as he might have done. Similarly, it may be helpful to know that Manon's deportation was no mere sensational adventure thought up by Prévost, but that such a form of punishment for 'fallen women' was still in use, albeit rarely, during the Regency. On questions such as these, where factual evidence can be adduced, any modern annotated edition of *Manon* should supply the reader with adequate details.

More tenuous, and often more important, are the current attitudes and assumptions about personal and social relationships. Certain notions would be taken for granted by Prévost and most of his contemporary readers; for instance, that financiers, however rich, are inherently inferior to men of noble birth. Rather than discuss these beliefs and assumptions in isolation, I shall deal with them as they arise in connection with a given character or event in the book.

There remains the question of literary background. Many twentieth-century novelists are both eclectic and experimental in their choice of narrative techniques, so that present-day readers may tend to assume that a given novelist tells his story in a certain way simply because he prefers that method. The eighteenth century too saw a good deal of experimentation in the novel; but Prévost's fiction is still conditioned and shaped, in some respects, by literary traditions. To understand why he adopted the specific narrative method that we find in *Manon*, we must take into account some of the conventions which prevailed in the fiction of the early eighteenth century.

We need first to remind ourselves that the full title of the work we are considering is: *Histoire du chevalier des Grieux et de Manon Lescaut*. The key-word here is *Histoire*, for the titles of eighteenth-century works of fiction generally convey not only the names of the protagonists, but also some fairly precise indication of the literary form in which the work was cast. As labels, specifying the nature of the goods they covered, eighteenth-century titles are nearly always more informative in this respect than the titles of nineteenth or twentieth-century novels. The title: *Julie ou la Nouvelle Héloïse, lettres de deux amants, habitants d'une petite ville au pied des Alpes, recueillies et publiées par Jean-Jacques Rousseau* may be somewhat lacking in crispness, but is rich in information. However, the first edition of this work, in 1761, did not even mention Julie or Héloïse on the title-page, which began: *Lettres de deux amants* . . . , as though what mattered most for prospective purchasers and readers was (apart from the name of Rousseau) the fact that this was a story told in letters.

The terms *Lettres* and *Mémoires* were precise and unambiguous as indications of literary forms, but as a title for fiction, *Histoire* had a wider range of senses. It could mean an independent story contained within a longer work. Both the long heroic romances of the seventeenth century and the memoir-novels which superseded them often allowed the hero to meet some minor personage who would proceed, on the slightest pretext or none at all, to relate his own adventures. This inter-polated narrative, practically always in the first person, would frequently be given its own heading in the text: *Histoire de* . . . . The *Avis de l'auteur* in *Manon Lescaut* begins: 'Quoique j'eusse pu faire entrer dans mes Mémoires les aventures du chevalier des Grieux . . .'. From this it is clear that the 'author' is referring to the convention of the *histoire* sandwiched into a long novel.

But another meaning had developed for the fictional *histoire*, a sense very close to that of the term *nouvelle* (from which the sense of the noun 'novel' in English has developed). The French *nouvelle* was in most cases a tale of recent times rather than of those remote historical periods found in the *roman héroïque*, and was generally a third-person narrative. Sometimes a group of such tales was published together, linked by a framework of narrative which described the occasion on which they were related. One such collection of tales calls for special mention in connection with *Manon Lescaut*. This is Robert Challes's *Les Illustres Françaises* (1713), in which an explanatory narrative frames seven longish stories. It seems extremely likely that Prévost had read this work, which was highly popular and went into numerous editions. These stories bear titles such as *Histoire de M. de Contamine et d'Angélique*; and Challes presents some of them as first-person narratives, while others are told in the third person.

So although the *Avis de l'auteur* implies that *Manon* belongs to the tradition of the interpolated *histoire*, and although the story was published as one volume of a long novel, this particular *Histoire* is in fact more akin to tales such as those in *Les Illustres Françaises*. The simplest way to explain the misleading nature of the opening remarks in the *Avis* is to retrace—using both facts and some plausible guesses—the order of events leading up to the publication of *Manon*.

We know that on arriving in Holland, Prévost's first task was to finish off the sequel and conclusion of the *Mémoires et aventures* (Volumes V and VI). In December 1730 he signed a contract to deliver to the printers by February 1st of the next year the manuscript of another long novel, *Le philosophe anglais ou histoire de monsieur Cleveland*, which was in all probability already well under way. But we can reasonably conjecture that at some point in December, 1730, or early January, 1731, he put his other work aside and wrote *Manon Lescaut*. Why he should have felt the desire or the need to compose the story at this particular point is something we may never know. But the mood and tone of *Manon* have much in common with the volumes of *Cleveland* which were published in 1731, a fact which bears out the supposition that they were written at about the same time.[2]

[2] For a more detailed discussion of this suggested chronology, see J. Sgard, *Prévost romancier* (Paris, Corti, 1968), pp. 228–32.

Let us suppose that Prévost's first version of *Manon* is simply Des Grieux's account of his tragic adventures, much as the story now stands, but without any introduction or intervention by the Man of Quality. Prévost now has the manuscript of a complete and independent *nouvelle*. And he is short of money—this we know for a fact. From his dealings with printers, he would know that when buying an author's manuscript they took into account not only quality but quantity. To offer *Manon* as part of the conclusion of the *Mémoires* would therefore make sense commercially. There would be far less attraction, for a printer, in an isolated little work which would not carry the cachet and appeal of the already popular *Mémoires*.

If the case was as I have outlined it, then Prévost would need to begin *Manon Lescaut* with a passage which contrived to suggest that the story did in some sense 'belong' to the *Mémoires*, and which also explained why it had not been inserted in the body of the book. This is exactly what is conveyed by the opening lines of the *Avis*. With a high-minded observation on the exigencies of relevance and literary structure (exigencies which he had already flouted in the *Mémoires*), capped by a quotation from Horace, Prévost blandly glosses over the fact that *Manon* is in no sense a part of the *Mémoires*. He has of course by now taken other steps to create some links between his *Histoire* and the earlier volumes. As we shall see, these links are tenuous; and this very fact has helped *Manon* to survive as a separate work.

It is the only work by Prévost which *has* survived, in the sense of still being familiar to a relatively wide reading public. Prévost was an extremely prolific man of letters who did not confine himself to writing novels: he translated a considerable number of works, including Richardson's *Clarissa Harlowe*; he edited and to a large extent wrote a journal, *Le Pour et Contre*; and he brought out a sixteen-volume *Histoire des Voyages*. We do not need to discuss why these works are now neglected by everyone except specialists of eighteenth-century French literature; the vast majority of books, in the normal way of things, fade and are forgotten. What requires explanation is the fact that *Manon* is not forgotten too. The work has always held its own in France, through all the fluctuating literary fashions. It has also been much translated, and has been adapted for the stage and the cinema.

One reason for this enduring popularity is that Prévost created, in *Manon*, a character who, like Faust or Don Juan, seems to embody the essence of a certain kind of human behaviour: Manon has become the archetype of the woman who is both fascinating and faithless. As such, she has caught the imagination of successive generations of readers. Moreover the work is short and its plot is simple and uncluttered— unlike the majority of Prévost's novels. There are further, more complex reasons, such as the way Prévost wins our sympathy for the narrator, the nature of his 'realism', and the qualities of his literary style. However, I shall study the book not by approaching it through such general problems, but by looking at the characters in turn, to see how each of them contributes to the pattern of the whole.

2. The Man of Quality: First Narrator and Moralist

Beginning in 1733, some printers took to issuing editions of *Manon Lescaut* as a separate work, quite apart from the *Mémoires et aventures d'un Homme de Qualité*. Since printers produced only such books as they thought would find buyers, we can safely deduce, firstly, that *Manon* was becoming a success with the reading public, and secondly, that it was thought to be satisfactory and comprehensible as an independent work. Yet both the *Avis* and the opening pages of the story proper are supposedly written by the 'author' of the *Mémoires*, that is, the Man of Quality himself. By the time that readers of the *Mémoires* reached Volume VII, they had become familiar with this character (whose name is given in Volume V as the Marquis de Renoncour), and had followed his course through life. So one might suppose that there would be some kind of loss for the reader who comes to *Manon Lescaut* without this preliminary knowledge. There is indeed a certain loss, but so minimal that its very slightness demonstrates how little *Manon Lescaut* has to do with the Marquis's life-story.

The openings of both the *Avis* and the *Première partie* refer back to the *Mémoires*. Those eighteenth-century readers who had not read the *Mémoires* would still, in all probability, recognize the reference. The modern reader, coming to *Manon* as a literary classic, will usually find a footnote supplying this information. The remainder of the *Avis* has no connection with the events of Renoncour's life. In the story itself, a few more sentences which lead up to the Marquis's second meeting with Des Grieux (pp. 15–16) again recall events in the *Mémoires*. And once more, a footnote will remedy any uncertainty in the reader's mind. Moreover, the reader knows that Des Grieux and Manon are the protagonists: it is *their* story we are preparing to enjoy. So these brief references to past actions of the narrator can be neglected, however puzzling they might seem.

Prévost has in fact glossed over, quite skilfully, one factor arising from the *Mémoires* which might well have caused complications. This is the presence, during the encounter of Des Grieux and Renoncour in Calais, of the latter's pupil, the Marquis de Rosemont. He is mentioned in passing: 'J'arrivais de Londres à Calais avec le marquis de . . . , mon élève' (p. 15). Renoncour addresses one remark to him, on recognizing Des Grieux in the street. Young Rosemont then fades from sight and memory except for the last paragraph of the *Première partie*, where the use of *nous* and *notre* makes it clear that he too has been listening to Des Grieux's story. Now Des Grieux tells the Man of Quality: 'Monsieur, vous en usez si noblement avec moi, que je me reprocherais, comme une basse ingratitude, d'avoir quelque chose de réservé pour vous' (p. 16). But he owes no such debt of gratitude to Rosemont, and we might wonder at his willingness to relate 'non seulement mes malheurs et mes peines, mais encore mes désordres et mes plus honteuses faiblesses' before a complete stranger, and one much of his own age.

Furthermore, in the context of the *Mémoires* this meeting in Calais is supposed to occur at a time when Renoncour, in his role as mentor, is trying to discourage Rosemont from giving way to passionate love. Was it wise of Renoncour, not knowing what conclusions Des Grieux's adventures might provide, to let his impressionable young pupil listen to these confidences?

These are the questions one might pertinently ask about a real-life situation, but they are irrelevant in this context. To a problem arising from a literary procedure, Prévost found a literary rather than a 'real-life' solution. The problem begins, I would suggest, with Prévost's decision to attach the story of Des Grieux and Manon, come what may, to the *Mémoires*. The simple, wholly conventional way of achieving this is to make Des Grieux tell the story to the Man of Quality. But why should he do so? Because they have met before, and Renoncour then showed him some kindness for which Des Grieux is grateful. These two meetings need, in terms of the *Mémoires*, to be spaced out; so the first is set at a moment of crisis—the eve of Manon's embarkation for America—and the second must of course come when the liaison has been ended, by her death. Between these meetings, two years or so will be required for the journeys to and from America and the events which happened there. So Prévost finds, in the *Mémoires*, two points in the already rather vague chronology of events where he can insert, in retrospect, the Man of Quality's encounters with Des Grieux. The second of these happens to fit conveniently enough into Renoncour's return from England but has the disadvantage that Rosemont is now travelling with him. Prévost's

solution? To establish Rosemont's presence, so that no niggling critic
can claim he has been forgotten; and then, in literary terms, to reduce
him to silence and nonentity, so that the reader will not be moved to
notice how unlikely or inappropriate he is as an extra listener for Des
Grieux. (We sometimes forget that an author's skill depends in part upon
what he does *not* mention.) On this occasion Prévost's sleight of hand—
Now you see him, now you don't—is admirable. (After all this, I should
emphasize that such a reconstruction of the literary processes involved
can be no more than a hypothesis; and that, even supposing the hypothesis to be valid, the skilful suppression of Rosemont may be something which Prévost accomplished without much conscious reflection.)

We are left with Renoncour himself in three distinct roles: as an
editor, whose preface points out the moral of the story which follows;
as a participant, at one stage, in the events of the story; and as the
listener-cum-chronicler who has recorded it for our benefit. In each of
these roles he is independent, in the sense that we can understand him
fully enough without knowing anything about his thoughts and actions
in earlier volumes of the *Mémoires*.

His presence as audience and recorder does not offer much opportunity for character-revelation. He becomes, at this stage, a functional
element in the presentation of the *Histoire*; any protagonist of a memoir-
novel would do as much, whatever his personality. We may merely note
in passing that he is made to offer the conventional guarantee as to the
authenticity and accuracy of his account:

> Je dois avertir le lecteur ici que j'écrivis son histoire presque aussitôt
> après l'avoir entendue, et qu'on peut s'assurer, par conséquent, que
> rien n'est plus exact et plus fidèle que cette narration. (p. 16)

Renoncour adds that he will leave the rest of the narrative entirely
to the Chevalier. In fact he does not keep this promise: at the end of the
first part he intervenes to suggest a break for supper. One might argue
that this reminder of Renoncour-as-listener is a slight blemish on the
work. By this stage some readers may well have forgotten the existence,
let alone the supposed presence, of the Man of Quality, and his
reappearance may cause a small shock of recall and readjustment
which could detract from the reader's absorption. Again, however, one
can see a literary reason for what Prévost has done here. There is one
point in Des Grieux's narrative where we shall *have* to be reminded of
Renoncour: their meeting at Pacy in the incident with which the novel

begins. The Chevalier's brief reference to this comes well towards the end of his story: 'Vous en fûtes témoin à Pacy. Votre rencontre fut un heureux moment de relâche . . .' (p. 182). If we had heard and seen nothing of Renoncour since p. 17, this reminder that he is sitting there listening might be even more of a shock. So his intervention at the end of the first part can be considered as a preparation for his reappearance towards the close of the tale. With the same end in view, the Chevalier is made, in the pages leading up to the encounter at Pacy in the second part, to address some remarks directly to the Man of Quality, using *vous*. One can see how Prévost has tried to integrate Renoncour-as-listener into the business of Des Grieux's story-telling.

As a listener, Renoncour has little individuality. The *Avis* and the opening of the novel do, however, provide sufficient material for a limited kind of characterization. The trouble is that the characters which emerge from the two passages would seem to be somewhat inconsistent, to say the least.

The point of comparison is Renoncour's reactions towards Des Grieux. At Pacy, the Man of Quality discovers a good deal about the Chevalier. He observes, for instance, that Des Grieux is of good birth and breeding; that he is ready to sacrifice his social advantages for love; that his behaviour—including the projected attack on the convoy—verges on the criminal; and that he accepts the likelihood of more terrible disasters to come. What all this amounts to is that after meeting the Chevalier and hearing his point of view at Pacy, Renoncour knows all the main elements of the description which he then set out in the *Avis*.

Now in this *Avis*, Des Grieux's story is summed up as 'un terrible exemple', and his actions are condemned. One might therefore expect that at Pacy, after learning so much of the Chevalier's character and intentions, Renoncour would have sought to restrain him, would have pointed out the reprehensible nature of his conduct, and tried to save him from 'les dernières infortunes'. Instead he judged Des Grieux's situation to be 'touching', gave him money to further his plans, and also gave money to the officer in charge of the convoy, to make things easier for Des Grieux. Can this be the same character, expressing lofty moral sentiments in the *Avis*, and condemning out of hand the very type of conduct which he had helped Des Grieux to pursue?

The two passages can hardly be reconciled. Is one of them more reliable than the other? Or to phrase the question differently, have we any reason to treat one of them as less reliable? To my mind, the *Avis* is clearly suspect; its whole purpose is to explain, excuse and defend. We have already seen that there is a certain speciousness about the way Prévost introduces this *Histoire*. The remainder of the *Avis* seeks to convince us of the high moral purpose which led the author to publish his story. This seems to me a case where the writer may well be putting up his defences because he expects to be attacked. Prévost was intelligent enough to realise that *Manon* might be severely censured on moral grounds—and such censure was indeed expressed by many critics. In my view, therefore, the *Avis* is largely a piece of special pleading, and as such to be treated with caution.

If we then conclude that we should accept Renoncour's help and encouragement for Des Grieux as a more reliable version of the Man of Quality's character, we are left with the puzzle that in the *Mémoires* he firmly tries to prevent young Rosemont from pursuing a love no less passionate and pitiful. The only way out of these inconsistencies is to recognize that the Renoncour of *Manon Lescaut* is not the 'same' character as in the *Mémoires*, but is a personage set up specifically to shape and account for Des Grieux's narrative. The fact that he is labelled *l'Homme de Qualité* is merely part of Prévost's attempt to link *Manon* to the *Mémoires*. And the final consequence of all this is that anyone who reads *Manon Lescaut* by itself is not really at a disadvantage from not having read the six volumes of the *Mémoires et aventures*.

It must also be admitted that most readers will not devote much critical attention to the Man of Quality, and may well fail to notice the inconsistencies between his moral pronouncements in the *Avis* and his actions at Pacy. In any case, the *Avis* is useful in one particular respect: it gives the impression of being written by an upright man of high moral principles, and this of course adds weight and conviction to the Man of Quality's comments on Manon and her lover.

Even if the *Avis* is described as merely a piece of special pleading which also happens to serve a useful literary purpose, it cannot be dismissed on these grounds alone from further consideration. Indeed, most critics who write on the moral import of *Manon Lescaut* take the *Avis* as their starting-point, and discuss the issues in the kind of terms which are proposed there. This is perhaps to allow too much importance to Prévost's own way of handling the subject. In general, modern critics are not unduly respectful towards the aims and intentions expressed by novelists: Balzac claimed to be a social historian, but is hardly considered as a reliable source-book for historians; Zola set out to make his novels 'scientific', but neither literary critics nor scientists take his 'scientific' ideas seriously. If Prévost, in the persona of the Man of Quality, presents himself as a moralist, why should we accept him at his own valuation? There are, obviously enough, some moral issues raised by the behaviour of Des Grieux and Manon. I suggest that we consider them as they arise, without reference to the kind of judgment Prévost offers. When we have drawn our own conclusions, we can turn back to the *Avis* and compare them with the views we find there.

On the level of literary expression, too, the *Avis* is not wholly satis-factory: the 'auteur' devotes a long and learned paragraph to making the relatively simple point that an interesting story may affect our ideas and actions in a way that no mere abstract statement of moral precepts can manage to do. By contrast, the Man of Quality's introduction to Des Grieux's narrative is, on the literary level, quite crisp and economical, and certainly effective.

A standard formula for the seventeenth-century 'heroic' novel was for the narrator to begin at an interesting point, well into the story, thus plunging the reader *in medias res*; after a while, some opportunity would be found for a flash-back, in which the hero explained how he had come to be in the crucial situation where the reader first met him. This device carried the prestige of being modelled on the great epic poems like the *Aeneid*. In contrast to this, most memoir-novels began at the moment when their hero or heroine could be considered adult (since childhood was held to be not worth describing), and then progressed straight on in time. In *Manon Lescaut*, Prévost has contrived a skilful blending of the two techniques. The Chevalier begins his story in a thoroughly conventional way: 'J'avais dix-sept ans.' But before he speaks these words, we have seen him involved in the strange situation at Pacy.

The observer who first presents him to us, the Man of Quality, has not met Des Grieux before, nor Manon, and might therefore be assumed to be impartial. Since he sees the young people as deserving of sympathy, the reader too may adopt this attitude.

This whole question of enlisting the reader's sympathy is extremely important for *Manon Lescaut*. Our ultimate verdict as to whether, in the simplest of terms, we like or dislike the novel may well depend to a large extent on Prévost's success, in this respect, with each individual reader. The Chevalier's own narrative carries the chief burden of this task, but it is interesting to see how the Man of Quality's narrative too,

short as it is, includes a number of touches calculated to make us feel
favourably inclined. We will discuss later on how his first impressions of
Des Grieux and Manon contribute to their characterization. For the
moment, let us consider the various hints and implications concerning
the Man of Quality himself.

This story reverts to a point in the *Mémoires* where he had chosen to
retire to a life of solitude, but was willing to disrupt this way of life
occasionally, in order to help his daughter. That is, he is an affectionate
father, prepared to put himself out for his daughter's sake. When he
arrives at Pacy and finds the excited crowd gathering outside the inn, he
gets one of the guards to tell him what is going on. But the guard's
laconic account does not arouse his curiosity or interest; it is only when
an old woman comes out, exclaiming about the pitiful sight and telling
Renoncour how heart-rending it is, that he takes the trouble to dis-
mount and go inside. In other words, he responds to an appeal to his
feelings, he shows *sensibilité*. We are then given further suggestions of
his kindness and readiness to sympathize with suffering. And the scene
ends with the only action he can take to help Des Grieux: the giving of
money. This generosity, the willingness to give freely with no thought
of obtaining anything for oneself in return, is a noble trait, to be contrasted with the bourgeois habit of expecting always to get something
for one's money. We see the generosity again when Renoncour meets
Des Grieux for the second time: observing that the Chevalier is not
'fort bien en argent', he arranges that the young man shall be put up at
the Lion d'Or and lack for nothing.

It is a scanty enough picture which emerges, revealed by implication
and actions rather than by overt statements. But if we take into account
the fact that this vignette follows the high moral sentiments of the *Avis*,
it seems clear that the Man of Quality is a person meant to be admired
and trusted. To that extent, his view of Manon and Des Grieux as
touching and appealing must influence us, and prepare us to receive
sympathetically the Chevalier's account of how he and Manon reached
such a pass of suffering and humiliation.

3. *Manon: The Enigmatic Heroine*

As early as 1742, one printer brought out an edition of the work entitled simply *Histoire de Manon*. In the twentieth century, popular editions of the novel generally bear the title: *Histoire de Manon Lescaut*; alternatively they may, like translations, be called *Manon Lescaut*. Even scholarly versions such as the two post-war Garnier editions have *Histoire de Manon Lescaut* as the running title at the top of their pages. And the two operas based on the story, by Massenet and Puccini, are called *Manon* and *Manon Lescaut* respectively.

Apart from the fact that *Des Grieux* is scarcely a catchy title for an opera, it is clear, from the way that Manon has usurped pride of place in the title, that she is generally viewed as the leading character. In all probability Prévost himself, when he wrote the work, did not see her in this light. The Man of Quality's outline of the story begins: 'J'ai à peindre un jeune aveugle . . .' (p. 4), and concentrates entirely on Des Grieux, with not a mention of Manon. And Prévost did, after all, imply a certain order of interest or importance when he chose to call the work: *Histoire du cheavlier des Grieux et . . .* He could conceivably have reversed the order of the names, or else omitted Des Grieux from the title completely; in 1740 he published another long *nouvelle* which is again the story of a man's doubts, fears and sufferings concerning the woman he loves, and this was entitled simply *Histoire d'une Grecque moderne*.

In one very simple sense it is somewhat paradoxical that Manon should be seen as the chief character: in terms of the amount of space explicitly devoted to her in the story, or the number of occasions she appears on the scene, her role is clearly less important than Des Grieux's. Moreover, by the very nature of the narrative form, we are constantly occupied with the Chevalier's thoughts and feelings, while the occasions when Manon reveals her own motives are more rare. Manon's domination of the story is thus a qualitative rather than a quantitative affair. Our first need is therefore to analyse what kind of a character Prévost has created in Manon and also, of course, the methods he uses for her portrayal.

In one very important respect, namely the effect that Manon creates upon men, Prévost relies largely upon implication and inference. Take

our very first glimpse of Manon, seen through the eyes of the Man of
Quality. He does provide one or two visual details, as well as mentioning
the feelings of respect and pity aroused in him. But what is more significant, even though it goes without comment, is that she is the only one
of the twelve women who captures his attention, and captures it
immediately: 'Parmi les douze filles qui étaient enchaînées six à six par le
milieu du corps, il y en avait une . . .' (p. 11). This 'one', we must infer, is
visibly superior to her companions, since the Man of Quality says not a
word about them. The comments of the chief guard show that he too—
insensitive as we may suppose him to be—is aware of her superiority:
'il me semble qu'elle vaut un peu mieux que ses compagnes' (p. 12).

This ability of Manon to create an immediately favourable impression
on any and every kind of man who sees her is the central factor not only
in Prévost's characterization but also in the structure of the plot. The
effect she has on Des Grieux is of course a *coup de foudre*: 'Elle me parut
si charmante que . . . je me trouvai enflammé tout d'un coup jusqu'au
transport' (p. 19). As for M. de B. . . , 'l'ayant vue à sa fenêtre, il était
devenu passionné pour elle' (p. 46). M. de G. . . M. . . has only to meet
her to be 'charmé de son mérite' (p. 71). The Italian prince, having seen
her out walking, considers her to be 'la plus charmante personne du
monde' (p. 119). If a man does not immediately appreciate her charms
and want her for his own, there is some good reason, in terms either of
his station in life or of his relationship to the Chevalier. Tiberge is
immune since he is both a cleric and a friend of Des Grieux. M. de T. . .
is likewise restrained by friendship, though after his first sight of Manon
he admits that he envies Des Grieux: 'Il n'y a point de sort glorieux
auquel je ne préférasse une maîtresse si belle et si passionnée' (p. 103).
The valet Marcel is of course too lowly to aspire to the possession of
Manon, much as he admires her. Hostility towards Manon, on the other
hand, occurs only in men who have tried to obtain her and failed, or in
men who have not actually met her. Des Grieux's father and—as far as
we know—the *Lieutenant général de Police*, who orders her deportation,
have never seen the woman they condemn.

It is clear, from the way Prévost relates her successive conquests, that
it is *seeing* Manon which matters; whatever her attractions may be in
the way of gaiety, wit, sympathy or passion, her appearance alone is
sufficient to arouse men's love or desire. But when we ask what Manon
looked like, we come to the point made by so many critics, that Prévost's
information on this score is exiguous to a degree. She is *belle*, there can

be no doubt of that. It is the single qualifying term used by the Man of Quality when he turns to the chief guard and asks for information about 'cette belle fille'. Des Grieux likewise, at an early stage of the love-affair, refers to Manon as 'ma belle maîtresse' (p. 21). However, Prévost never supplies any descriptive detail of this beauty. Whether her eyes were blue or brown, whether her nose was classical or retroussé, we are never told. This might be seen as a brilliant piece of tactful omission by Prévost. Manon's ability to fascinate every man in sight goes beyond the ordinary powers of beauty; it has a touch of myth or fairy-tale. Hers is not so much the beauty of Helen of Troy as of Circe or *La Belle Dame sans Merci*. For it is noticeable that terms like *charme* and *charmant* recur in reports of her effect on others, and these words still carried, at the time, a strong association with the notion of spells and enchantment. To try and convey such beauty in terms of any precision—fine-arched eyebrows, lustrous blonde hair, a well-turned ankle and so forth—would be to reduce it to mundane measurable specifications and would limit the scope of the reader's imagination.

However, it is unlikely that the omission sprang from a simple conscious decision on the writer's part, such as: 'I will leave Manon's appearance undefined so that every reader can visualize his own ideal of feminine beauty'. Several trends of seventeenth-century thought, still influential in the early eighteenth century, stressed the importance of the spiritual, mental and emotional aspects of mankind as compared with the 'mere' body. The religious contribution of Christianity is obvious; Cartesian philosophy and psychology could be made to bear the same message; the Platonic idealism taken to excess by some of the *précieuses* also played down the physical aspects of life. Ideas of this kind were common coin amongst educated people, including of course authors. And such notions were reflected in the practice of writers who aspired to create serious works of literature. It was thus a matter of literary convention that detailed description of a character's appearance was the exception rather than the rule. Prévost usually takes this approach; only rarely does he provide information to help the reader visualize a character, and when he does it may be because, as in the case of the Dean of Coleraine, that person suffers from physical peculiarities and disabilities. His reticence about Manon's appearance therefore represents no departure from his usual practice. It is moreover quite in keeping that a young man educated as Des Grieux has been should refrain from particularizing about the details of his mistress's beauty.

This brief and necessarily over-simplified discussion must already have suggested that the kinds of ideas accepted and taken for granted by many writers of the period are the very reverse of what we understand by 'realism' in works of the nineteenth and twentieth centuries. A further aspect of realism which differentiates modern novels from serious eighteenth-century works is the treatment of sex and love-making. An aesthetic concept which complemented the religious and philosophic ideas outlined above was that of *bienséance*, the adherence to what is proper and fitting. In the case of serious works of art, as distinct from the purely comic or satiric, this involved the observance of strict standards of decorum and refinement. Overt discussion, let alone description, of so primitive an activity as physical love-making was out of the question. We have become so accustomed to increasing freedom and explicitness in the literary treatment of sex that we may be misled by Prévost's reticence on this topic. His allusions to the physical relationship between the Chevalier and Manon tend to be discreet in the extreme. An outstanding example is his brief reference to the first night which the lovers spend together:

> Nos projets de mariage furent oubliés à Saint-Denis; nous fraudâmes les droits de l'Église, et nous nous trouvâmes époux sans y avoir fait réflexion. (p. 25)

This elliptical and euphemistic style of expression should not blind us to the fact that the Chevalier's love is based on physical attraction and his happiness depends on the continuing and sole physical possession of Manon. He may go on, in the passage just quoted, to praise 'son esprit, son cœur, sa douceur', but these are not the qualities which first enchanted him, or which would in the last resort sustain his passion. The thought of another man making love to her is his particular torment; there is something doubly ironic about the fact that he is just about to exercise poetic justice on young G... M... by getting into his bed with Manon, when the elder G... M... arrives to have him arrested, according to the laws of a harsher and more mundane justice. The relative delicacy with which Prévost refers to such matters was increased when he revised the text of *Manon Lescaut* in 1753. Where, for instance, the 1731 version had said: 'l'heure de se coucher étant arrivée, il proposa à Manon d'aller au lit' (p. 224), the new, more refined text said: 'Enfin, l'heure du sommeil étant arrivée, il parla d'amour et d'impatience' (p. 77). (We shall need to return to this question of Prévost's revision of the text.)

While physical love is all-important to the Chevalier, to Manon it is far less so. One might argue, albeit in a somewhat quixotic fashion, that her view of love is purer and more idealized than his, since she can dissociate her feelings from the physical aspects of passion and is prepared to continue 'loving' him while becoming the mistress of another man. But it is lack of thought rather than subtle conceptualizing which leads to such an attitude on Manon's part. So we must now go beyond her surface beauty and try to analyse, largely through her behaviour, the kind of character which Prévost has built up, and the springs of her conduct.

There is an apparent gulf between Manon's appearance and her actions. The traits which first impress the Man of Quality are the nobility of her mien, the respect and pity she arouses in him, and her modesty in trying to avoid the gaze of the curious spectators. Noble, modest, worthy of respect and pity—can these be appropriate terms for the Manon we shall see attempting to defraud the elder M. de G. . . M. . . of money and jewels, or insisting gaily that Des Grieux shall eat young G. . . M. . .'s supper and sleep in his bed? The answer, in Prévost's terms, is that these good qualities are innate in her, and could develop fully under favourable circumstances. The Chevalier is made to subscribe to an 'essentialist' psychology, as opposed to the Existentialist approach. For the latter, one's personality and one's existence are inseparable, in the sense that every choice and every action in one's life contribute to one's character. So not until the moment of death is one's character 'complete'; for the living there is always the possibility of new choices which could alter one's character. The 'essentialist', on the other hand, holds that one is born with certain qualities which are the real basis (or essence) of one's character. One may be forced to act in ways which seem to contradict these qualities, but if other people form character-judgments on the grounds of such actions, they will be taking a purely superficial view. The Man of Quality and the Chevalier show a more profound insight when they recognize that *Manon* is 'essentially' noble and virtuous.

Unfortunately Manon possesses, as well as her good qualities, a further less creditable trait, her love of pleasure. It is this, combined with the Chevalier's poverty, which inhibits the free exercise of her basically virtuous tendencies. The Chevalier analyses this overwhelming need for pleasure in a crucial passage beginning: 'Manon était une créature d'un caractère extraordinaire' (p. 61). He clarifies the point:

'C'était du plaisir et des passetemps qu'il lui fallait.' She must be kept amused and entertained; boredom is the one intolerable bugbear.

Is this characteristic really so 'extraordinary' as the Chevalier states? If a woman can lead a life of leisure, devoid of responsibilities, and has no particular taste for pastimes which can occupy her in solitude— reading, sewing, painting and the like—then it seems only too likely that she will be eager for balls, the theatre, card-playing and parties of pleasure of every kind. The same remark applies, *mutatis mutandis*, to men, and when we consider Rousseau's strictures on Parisian society, or the life led by Crébillon's Meilcour and Laclos's Valmont, we may conclude that the quest for amusement was by no means uncommon. Such a taste was, however, inappropriate for Manon, since she had not been born into the leisured aristocracy.

If we are to grasp her character we must also take into account two other traits: her lack of foresight and her lack of moral principles. Manon seems usually to be incapable of foreseeing, or unwilling to take seriously, the consequences of her actions. When she agrees to become the mistress of the elder G... M..., she does not realize how deeply this will wound Des Grieux. Having discovered his reaction to her plan, she changes her mind. But she then decides to run off with the money and jewels she has received from G... M..., paying no attention to the fact that a rich and powerful man of this kind can arrange for her to be caught and punished. When history repeats itself, to the extent that they have the chance to cheat young G... M... of his gifts, Manon again urges the plan upon Des Grieux. This time the details of the trick had been devised by M. de T..., But Manon 'ne trouvait rien de si joli que ce projet' (p. 149). For a young woman who had already been incarcerated, such light-hearted running of further risks is foolhardy to a degree.

Linked with her lack of foresight is a complete absence of any moral scruples. Her actions are never conceived as involving moral issues, only in terms of expediency for producing a desired result. For her, clearly enough, moral principles have no relevance or meaning: she is not immoral, but amoral. This is why she can write to the Chevalier, in the same sentence, 'Tu es l'idole de mon cœur', and, 'Dans l'état où nous sommes réduits c'est une sotte vertu que la fidélité' (p. 69). The concept of faithfulness as a virtue, or of 'virtue' itself in any absolute sense, is something beyond her grasp. One may further note that since Manon has no moral principles, there is never any question of her 'yielding to temptation' in a religious or ethical sense. The Chevalier is left as the only one who is beset by temptation and aware of the issues involved.

We have observed in Manon three salient traits: the need to be amused, the lack of foresight and the absence of moral standards. These, in my view, combine to provide a coherent enough portrait of someone with the outlook of a child rather than an adult. In modern jargon, one could describe Manon as emotionally immature (her physical maturity is certainly not in question). There is nothing inconsistent or surprising in Des Grieux, as well as other men, being fascinated by this combination of adult feminine beauty and childlike irresponsibility.

The trouble is that Manon also possesses sufficient strength of character to impose her will upon the Chevalier. Occasionally Des Grieux acts on his own initiative, to keep Manon or win her back. But in the crucial episodes which lead to disaster, it is Manon who takes the first step or imposes her will. At Amiens she claims that the Chevalier is her cousin (with a quickness of deceit which surprises Des Grieux and augurs none too well for the future); this enables the young couple to plan their flight. In Paris she accepts the offers of M. de B. . . without consulting Des Grieux. And a year later it is she who revives the liaison by coming to Saint-Sulpice. After their reconciliation, Des Grieux says: 'Je lui demandai quel nouvel ordre elle jugeait à propos de mettre dans nos affaires' (p. 47). Manon takes the decisions, and the Chevalier responds with: 'Je consentis à toutes ses volontés sans réplique.' Here, at its clearest, is a reversal of the traditional masculine and feminine roles: Manon seeks him out, wins back his love, carries him off, and provides money for them both to live on. As the story proceeds, some of Des Grieux's actions are—through force of circumstance—more decisive and more under his own control. But he is still incapable of denying Manon anything she has set her heart on: when she adopts the 'joli projet' against young G. . . M. . . , we find the Chevalier saying: 'Je cédai à ses instances, malgré les mouvements secrets de mon cœur' (p. 150). The Chevalier is weak as parents are weak when they give way to a spoilt child. Like such parents, he ignores the future evils that may come from acceding to the importunate requests, and prefers the immediate gratification of smiles and delight instead of reproaches and tears.

Characters and actions such as those of the Chevalier and Manon Lescaut do not seem to me at all implausible. (Whether we like or approve of such people is of course quite another question.) And this verdict on Manon's plausibility raises one final point about her as a literary creation: Prévost was being realistic, daring and relatively original when he portrayed, in a serious work, the situation of a noble, well-educated, hitherto virtuous young man falling a victim to the love of a woman who was morally unworthy of him. Realistic, because we must surely allow that such liaisons do occur in real life. Daring and original, because such a situation had only rarely been used as material for a serious story. There are plenty of pretty women in humorous tales, from Boccaccio onwards, who can twist an otherwise sensible man round their fingers and then betray or cuckold him. It was the development of the non-comic *nouvelle* which made way for the change, since here the potentially shocking or scandalous situations of contemporary life could be explored in all their serious or tragic implications. In Challes's *Les Illustres Françaises* Prévost would find a story in which a noble young man, Des Frans, fell victim to the attractions of the scheming and unworthy Silvie—though as things turn out we find that appearances were against her, and she was really worthy of his love. Prévost would seem to have taken the situation to its limit, for Manon is indeed the unprincipled girl she seems. It is as though Prévost had set himself a challenge, to write a story of passionate love, leading to immorality and degradation, and to present it in a way which would nevertheless engage the reader's sympathy. In this chapter we have looked at Manon with a calm and critical eye. But while we are actually reading *Manon Lescaut*, we are given no chance for such dispassionate analysis, since the Chevalier, through whom the story reaches us, is the voice of passion pleading its own cause.

4. Des Grieux: Narrator and 'Âme sensible'

Manon Lescaut is one of a small class of works which present a special problem to the critic. While it is true that there is always a qualitative difference between the experience of reading a work of literature and that of critical analysis of the same work, these two kinds of experience are not usually conflicting or contradictory. One can discuss *Candide* without pausing to laugh at its wit, or *Phèdre* without feeling again its tragic tensions; but such discussion would not deny Voltaire his wit or lead to the conclusion that Phèdre was not a tragic figure. By contrast, we may be carried along by, and endorse, the ideas and actions of characters such as Valmont in Laclos's *Les Liaisons dangereuses* as long as we are absorbing the work itself, but reject these ideas and actions when we stand back to consider the work critically. Sometimes the disagreement is on a trivial level: we can read a James Bond story with interest and excitement, but put it down with a sigh when we come to the end, recognizing that it is a fantasy and that the real-life business of spying has no such glamour. The more serious conflicts or disagreements are on the levels of thought which involve ethical judgments. The fiction presents one kind of moral outlook, which is to some extent convincing while we are reading the book; but once we move on to critical assessment, away from the aesthetic experience, we find that this moral outlook is not compatible with our personal, real-life standards.

Manon Lescaut is, by virtue of its narrative form, an extreme case of this problem. The Chevalier and Manon argue and behave in ways which most of us would be ready to condemn as anti-social, immoral, criminal, etc., if we were to meet them in real life; but we experience these arguments and actions for the first time through the Chevalier's narration of them. They are described for us from his point of view, coloured with his emotions. If we enjoy the book and become involved in the progress of the action, this means, almost inevitably, that we feel some sympathy with Des Grieux and can share his point of view. If, on completing the story, we stand back and judge the Chevalier unfavourably, we should keep in mind that this *is* a later reaction, not the one inspired by the aesthetic experience itself.

The possibility of these conflicting reactions, however obvious it may seem, needs spelling out in detail because the whole of the Chevalier's story is a *plaidoyer*, explaining and justifying his behaviour. He admits his offences and pleads guilty—but with extenuating circumstances. If we were jurymen in a court case, it would be our duty to reject immediately anything specious or false in his arguments. While reading such a work of art, however, we should perhaps be less sceptical, more willing to co-operate. The time for critical appraisal will come later.

Prévost himself was fully aware of the power of a skilled author to persuade the reader out of his customary beliefs. When discussing a memoir-novel by Mesnier, he pointed out that:

> L'art suprême dans un livre de cette nature consiste sans doute à se rendre ainsi maître de l'attention et du goût des lecteurs, indépendamment de la vérité des faits qu'on leur raconte.[1]

Manon is 'un livre de cette nature' insofar as Prévost tries to convince us that it is a true story about real people. And one should note that he speaks of the novelist controlling not only the attention of the reader, but also his *goût*, or value-judgments. Furthermore, the supposed 'author's' point of view may be distorted by his own emotions: a man in love can hardly be expected to write in an impartial and objective way about his beloved. In the opening paragraph of *Histoire d'une Grecque moderne* there is a kind of *caveat lector*, drawing the reader's attention to this risk:

> Je suis l'amant de la belle Grecque dont j'entreprends l'histoire. Qui me croira sincère dans le récit de mes plaisirs ou de mes peines? Qui ne se défiera point de mes descriptions et de mes éloges? Une passion violente ne fera-t-elle point changer de nature à tout ce qui va passer par mes yeux ou par mes mains? En un mot, quelle fidélité attendra-t-on d'une plume conduite par l'amour?

Still more specific, because it shows the precise use that a novelist can make of his mastery over the unwary reader, is a passage from the *Mémoires et aventures* themselves. Comparing the heroic novels with the more recent vogue 'd'histoires amoureuses et de nouvelles galantes', the Man of Quality blames this new type of fiction:

> En voulant peindre les hommes au naturel, on y fait un portrait trop charmant de leurs défauts; et loin que de pareilles images puissent

[1] *Le Pour et Contre*, 1738, XVI, 357.

inspirer la haine du vice, elles en cachent la difformité pour le faire aimer.[2]

The chief task in discussing Des Grieux is therefore to discover what kinds of art Prévost employed to make him a persuasive and convincing narrator, capable, for some readers at least, of winning sympathy for notions they would normally condemn.

Since we are to hear the whole story from Des Grieux's lips, the author must clearly do his best to make him an attractive character. He is a young man, a mere seventeen at the point when his adventures begin and only five years or so older when he relates them to the Man of Quality. He is good-looking and intelligent. It is not always easy for a novelist to make his first-person narrator convey such flattering details without also making him sound conceited, but Prévost has handled this matter quite skilfully. First, of course, we are shown Des Grieux through the eyes of Renoncour, who is favourably impressed by his appearance. Most of the subsequent comments on the Chevalier's looks arise plausibly, and also show us other people's view of him. Lescaut sees his 'figure avantageuse' as an asset he could exploit by getting some elderly lady to keep him as a *cicisbeo* (p. 56). The guild of card-sharpers likewise appreciate the *gentillesse* of his face (p. 62). And Manon provides the final proof, when she offers the Italian prince a mirror and tells him—in terms which arouse comic echoes of Hamlet's 'Look here, upon this picture, and on this'—to judge how little chance he stands against the attractions of Des Grieux (p. 123).

As for Des Grieux's intelligence, his opening paragraph, designed to emphasize his initial ignorance about women and love, mentions his successful school career; and he later says that in his studies at Saint-Sulpice, 'je fis des progrès extraordinaires en peu de mois' (p. 42). Here the comment does not suggest bragging for its own sake: what will emerge is the fact that he is abandoning, for Manon, a way of life in which he could clearly succeed by his intellectual ability. Nor is he merely a bookworm; he can use his wits to good purpose when it comes to working out a method of escape from Saint-Lazare.

As well as good looks and intelligence, the Chevalier has a pleasing personality. The only people who are hostile to him are those men who wish to buy Manon's favours for themselves. Apart from them, Des

[2] *Mémoires et aventures d'un Homme de Qualité*, Paris, 1728, II, 81 (quoted in G. May, *Le dilemme du roman* (Paris Presses universitaires, 1963), p. 72).

Grieux can rely on the affection of his father and of Tiberge, and he has no difficulty in making new friends and allies such as M. de T. . . and the Man of Quality.

One of the traits which links the Chevalier and M. de T. . . in swift friendship is that both are men of feeling. Des Grieux is proud of the strength and variety of his emotions, and manifests them freely, especially in weeping. This particular aspect of his reactions is one that might be expected to appeal to many eighteenth-century readers, though in the twentieth century it is perhaps more likely to provoke blame or laughter. It is a part of the much wider phenomenon, in literature and in life, of sensibility.

In a brief study such as this, there is room for only an outline of the salient points about sensibility. The general concept is bound up with a certain view of human nature, in which the emotions, and particularly certain kinds of emotion, are seen as admirable and as adjuncts to virtue. In seventeenth-century Europe the partisans of various important religious doctrines—Puritanism, Calvinism, Jansenism—maintained a different position, generally arguing that the emotions were likely to be a source of sin, and should therefore be kept in check. The first manifestations of sensibility in French literature appear in a handful of stories published in the last decade of the seventeenth century. The tendency gathered way as the eighteenth century progressed, and in France the 1760s and 1770s were probably the apogee of this glorification of emotion in literature. The emotions most favoured were those concerned with sympathy and kindness, and the Man of Feeling was ultra-sensitive not only to the sufferings of others, but also to his own. Since it was creditable to experience such vivid emotional reactions, it was also praiseworthy and fashionable to show them—hence the sighs and tears and swooning that invaded much French (and English) literature in the mid-eighteenth century.

Some qualifying comments need to be made. Firstly, sensibility has a more respectable intellectual basis than we might be led to suppose from a mere acquaintance with over-sentimental characters in fiction. It has a grounding in seventeenth-century psychology: the emotions originate in the soul (which in Cartesian terms can be more or less equated with the conscious mind), and their scope and force therefore provide evidence of the soul's breadth and importance. Secondly, at no time, in the realm of literature, was sensibility more than one tendency among several. There were always some authors who ignored the trend and wrote seriously but without sentimental effusions; and there were many others who were ready to poke fun at *sensiblerie*. (Voltaire is an example of a writer who did occasionally show sensibility, but more often mocked it.) Even during the time when a large proportion of the new novels being published were full of *sensibilité*, the printers and booksellers were also re-editing earlier works of a comic, or at least less tearful, nature.

Thirdly, sensibility was undoubtedly a real-life phenomenon as well as a literary vogue. Biographies, letters and journals of the time show that some people did exalt the merits of the softer emotions, and displayed them too. There is no way of accurately assessing how widespread such attitudes and behaviour were; but since literature, in all probability, played its part in the process, we can perhaps assume that sensibility was favoured chiefly by the educated classes; there is something incongruous in the notion of the average *paysan* or valet or fishwife giving way to fainting fits or delicious floods of tears. But one must add that the ideas of the prosperous and powerful classes do tend to filter down and be imitated by the less fortunate.

The question of the spread of such notions brings us to a final point: however ridiculous *sensibilité* may seem in some of its uninhibited literary manifestations, it did contribute in real life to the growth and acceptance of certain concepts such as humanitarianism, philanthropy and social justice which most of us now take for granted as ideals. We should therefore not be too swift to condemn it. If we are fully to appreciate and enjoy eighteenth-century literature, we shall often need to make the effort of imagination to understand sensibility in its own terms. This is not to say that we should, even if we could, learn to feel and think like a Prévost or a Rousseau. What we can perhaps do is to restrain or suspend something of the adverse reaction we may tend to feel towards these tearful heroes and heroines.

Admittedly such restraint may be difficult when we read works like *Manon Lescaut*, for sensibility not only comes out in the characters' actions but also impregnates the literary expression. Grammatical construction is affected: there are more exclamations, apostrophes and rhetorical questions than we expect to find in a modern first-person narrative. Utterances of this kind can be seen, for instance, when Des Grieux reproaches Manon after her third betrayal:

Ah! Manon, lui dis-je d'un ton tendre, infidèle et parjure Manon! par où commencerai-je à me plaindre? . . .

C

Dieux! de quels mouvements n'étais-je point agité! Ah! Manon,
Manon, repris-je . . .

Inconstante Manon, repris-je encore, fille ingrate et sans foi, où
sont vos promesses et vos serments? Amante mille fois volage et
cruelle, qu'as-tu fait de cet amour que tu me jurais encore aujourd'hui?
(p. 141)

Expressions such as these are clearly influenced by the language and style
of classical French tragedy, a point to which we shall return.

Another method used to convey the strength of sensations and
emotions is the use of superlatives, hyperbole and various other forms of
emphasis.

Je me trouve le plus malheureux des tous les hommes, par cette même
constance dont je devais attendre le plus doux de tous les sorts et les
plus parfaites récompenses de l'amour. (p. 25)

The same tendency to prefer strong and emphatic expressions can be
seen in the choice of nouns and verbs suggesting extremes. When things
go wrong, the Chevalier is reduced at once to *désespoir*, his sufferings are
never less than *tourments*, his anger is a *transport de fureur*.

The general effect of these various linguistic traits is to produce a style
in which, by modern standards, the reactions seem exaggerated. So
while, as we noticed earlier, Prévost's treatment of sexual themes is
discreet and verbally reticent, his manner of conveying emotions goes
to the other extreme.

As these brief stylistic comments suggest, sensibility is woven into the
very fabric of *Manon Lescaut*. Only occasionally, in snatches of practical
detail for instance, does Prévost depart from this tone. And the pre-
dominant effect is perfectly in keeping with the personality of the
narrator, since Des Grieux is *une âme sensible*, and glories in the fact. He
is made to set out quite clearly his own belief in the superiority of sensitive souls:

Le commun des hommes n'est sensible qu'à cinq ou six passions, dans
le cercle desquelles leur vie se passe, et où toutes leurs agitations se
réduisent. Otez-leur l'amour et la haine, le plaisir et la douleur, l'es-
pérance et la crainte, ils ne sentent plus rien. Mais les personnes d'un
caractère plus noble peuvent être remuées de mille façons différentes; il
semble qu'elles aient plus de cinq sens, et qu'elles puissent recevoir des
idées et des sensations qui passent les bornes ordinaires de la nature;
et comme elles ont un sentiment de cette grandeur qui les élève au-
dessus du vulgaire, il n'y a rien dont elles soient plus jalouses. (p. 81)

From this very important passage we see that individuals can be graded according to their ability to 'feel'—in every sense. Although Des Grieux begins by talking only of the emotions, he goes on to discuss 'des idées et des sensations', which are accessible only to exceptional beings. This means that the truly sensitive man is literally made of finer stuff than the rest of mankind: his organs of perception are more finely attuned, his mind is more apt to embrace unusual ideas, and his emotions are more varied in range, more subtle in their nuances, and more profound in their effects. This superiority makes him truly 'noble'. This term, contrasted as it is with 'le commun des hommes' and 'le vulgaire', suggests a hierarchy. And in Des Grieux's world people are indeed classed and categorized by their rank in the hierarchy of sensibility. The guards at Pacy are 'lâches coquins' because they have the inhumanity to prevent Des Grieux talking to Manon. Tiberge is one of the élite, since he is attached to Des Grieux with 'une tendresse extraordinaire'. M. de T. . . is also accepted as truly noble, since he proves himself immediately to be 'tendre et généreux'. But perhaps the most interesting example is Marcel, the servant who helps to bring about Manon's escape from the Hôpital. The Chevalier says of him:

> Ce garçon avait l'âme moins basse et moins dure que ses pareils. Il avait été témoin de notre entrevue; ce tendre spectacle l'avait touché. (p. 104)

Marcel is sufficiently superior to his fellows to be able to feel sympathy for Manon and Des Grieux. But he cannot of course be expected to be really 'noble', so it is the Chevalier's liberal tip which finally clinches his loyalty.

The grading in Des Grieux's scale of sensibility is, we can see, closely related to the social class-system. In terms of expectations or probabilities, one can expect an aristocrat by birth to be fully *sensible* and therefore *noble*—though there will be exceptions. At the other end of the scale, a working-class man is not expected to be able to share in the finer feelings, but again one may meet, even at this level, a few people who can rise somewhat above their social status. Outrageously simple as this view of humanity may seem, we should remember, firstly, that Prévost's own ideas were not necessarily as simple; and secondly, that in the early eighteenth century there were still plenty of people in France—possibly a majority—who believed that aristocrats did tend to be superior, by birth as well as education, and that the vulgar were, with only a few exceptions, inherently less able and less sensitive than their 'betters'.

So far, the theories and modes of expression which we have found Prévost attributing to Des Grieux are comparable with other fictional characters of the period who evince sensibility, such as Marivaux's Marianne. But as part of his persuasive or justifying technique, the Chevalier is made to take his grading of mankind even a stage further in simplification: the noble and admirable people, together with those who like Marcel show some glimmerings of *sensibilité*, are all characters who are well-disposed towards the Chevalier and favour his plans to live with Manon. Tiberge comes into this group because, although he disapproves of Des Grieux's liaison, he never takes any action against it, and even helps the Chevalier with loans of money. At the other end of the scale are those people who disrupt the liaison, headed of course by the ignoble rich men who seduce Manon away from Des Grieux by gifts and promises. The elderly M. de G. . . M. . . illustrates the workings of the Chevalier's criteria. When he visits Des Grieux in Saint-Lazare, the latter's comments are at first not unfavourable:

> Je lui trouvai l'air plus grave et moins sot qu'il ne l'avait eu dans la maison de Manon. Il me tint quelques discours de bon sens sur ma mauvaise conduite. (p. 84)

When M. de G. . . M. . . reveals, however, that Manon, at his instigation, has been sent to the Hôpital, the case is altered. Des Grieux's subsequent explanation of why he lost his temper and attacked M. de G. . . M. . . contains phrases such as 'la plus horrible cruauté', 'la plus détestable de toutes les barbaries', 'l'action que l'indigne G. . . M. . . a eu la lâcheté de commettre' (p. 86).

The most striking case of all, in this respect, is Des Grieux's father. When the Chevalier's pleas for understanding produce their desired effect, we have a paragraph beginning: 'Un cœur de père est le chef d'œuvre de la nature' (p. 163). But when, in their next conversation, the father refuses to try and save Manon from being deported, Des Grieux quits him with a cry of: 'Adieu, père barbare et dénaturé'. His father has not enough sensitivity to appreciate Des Grieux's love for Manon, and is therefore reduced to the level of the savage in spite of his apparent rank of nobility.

Des Grieux himself would seem to present a contradiction in terms: he maintains that his own sensibility puts him among those who are noble, yet his actions—card-sharping, murder and so forth—are anything but noble. Such behaviour even disqualifies him, in a way, from being *sensible*, for he rarely shows any consideration for the feelings or welfare of anyone except Manon; besides cheating and killing, he holds up the kindly Père-Supérieur at gun-point, and frequently borrows money from the none-too-rich Tiberge. Similarly, while praising openness and sincerity as virtues of the noble heart, he frequently lies, to Tiberge as well as to lesser folk like the cab-driver or the ship's captain.

The notion which explains or excuses such conduct, in Des Grieux's system of beliefs, is that love is a privileged emotion. It is fundamentally innocent and natural, and by virtue of its importance it outweighs lesser feelings such as sympathy and consideration for others. The hero of *Cleveland* is made to present a quasi-philosophical defence of love as a natural right:

> Il me parut, après un sincère examen, que les droits de la nature étant les premiers de tous les droits, rien n'était assez fort pour prescrire contre eux; que l'amour en était un des plus sacrés, puisqu'il est l'âme de tout ce qui existe; et qu'ainsi tout ce que la raison et l'ordre établi parmi les hommes pouvaient faire contre lui, était d'en interdire certains effets sans pouvoir jamais le condamner dans sa source.[3]

This argument clearly envisages the possibility of the 'natural right' of love coming into conflict with the established usages of society—'l'ordre établi parmi les hommes'. Such a conflict does arise in the case of Des Grieux and Manon, but the Chevalier himself is not made to describe his troubles explicitly as a struggle with Society. He does, however, behave as though love should take precedence over any other consideration in his relationships with other people, and life with Manon becomes an end which justifies any means.

The strength of this motivation and its power to make Des Grieux neglect conventional standards of behaviour is already suggested by his conduct when he first meets Manon and runs away with her. During the subsequent period at his home and his year of study at Saint-Sulpice, love seems to have fallen into abeyance, but the reappearance of Manon is enough to revive its full force. There has, however, been a development in the interval: the Chevalier has become wiser by one piece of knowledge, that Manon requires pleasure and will, if need be, sell herself to any man with enough money to keep her entertained. This is a certainty which, apart from a few sanguine moments, is to stay with him

[3] *Le Philosophe anglais* . . . , Amsterdam, 1731, I, 197.

as long as they are in France. And at first, it seems to afford a guarantee that he can also overcome his love for her. 'Il est certain que je ne l'estimais plus' (p. 36), he says after learning how she had connived with M. de B. . . to have him carried off from Paris. And a little later, when planning his tranquil future way of life, he remarks: 'Comme je sens assez que mon cœur ne désirera que ce qu'il estime, j'aurai aussi peu d'inquiétudes que de désirs' (p. 40). This prophecy shows how little he knows himself. Not until Manon comes to see him at Saint-Sulpice does he realize that he can and does love her without being able to respect her moral standards. One can argue that from this point onwards there is little or no development in Des Grieux's character. He is consistently settled both in his knowledge of Manon's capacity for betraying him, and in his awareness of his own determination to try and keep her, come what may. The 'accidents' which ensue, such as the two occasions when they lose all their capital by fire and theft, are merely specific events which lead him into dishonesty and crime. But he has already proved himself capable of this kind of action when he agrees, on running away from Saint-Sulpice, to live on the money and jewels which Manon had received from M. de B. . . The increasing ignominy and crime into which he descends thus do no more than realize certain potentialities inherent in the situation of a young man like himself being helplessly in love with a girl like Manon.

In using the word 'helplessly', we are endorsing the Chevalier's own point of view. Already when at Saint-Sulpice he accepts her excuses for the first betrayal, he exclaims: 'Où trouver un barbare qu'un repentir si vif et si tendre n'eût pas touché?' (p. 47). Since he is anything but *barbare*, he cannot help but be swept off his feet, for the second time, by love. Similarly, when he agrees to take up card-sharping, it is only because no other solution is possible: 'Quelque répugnance que j'eusse à tromper, je me laissai entraîner par une cruelle nécessité' (p. 62).

This notion, that the Chevalier has no choice, that he is driven or compelled into his various crimes, is the key-stone of the whole elaborate structure of his defence. His inability to resist love, and his consequent overwhelming desire to keep Manon with him, are accounted for in two ways. On the one hand it is his own nature which produces such a state of affairs: it is because he is *sensible* rather than *barbare* that he must perforce succumb to Manon's charm. On the other hand, external forces drive him on: this love is 'written in the stars', it is Fate or Destiny which

DES GRIEUX   39

has established his inevitable course, and against such powers one cannot rebel.

The frequent use of terms such as 'l'ascendant de ma destinée', 'mon mauvais sort', 'un amour fatal' and so on, offers a skilful combination of two elements which could appeal to the reader and surreptitiously win his support. Firstly there is the reference to various notions which the sceptical mind dismisses as 'superstitious', 'unscientific', etc. But even in twentieth-century Europe a surprising number of people, while claiming to accept Christianity and the standards of modern science, still read and give some credence to the astrology column in their daily paper, still consider certain actions such as breaking a mirror to be 'unlucky', still hold that if someone escapes from a serious accident it was because he was not 'fated' to die just then. Beliefs of this kind were undoubtedly more widespread and powerful in Prévost's own time, and could be accepted more easily as a part of the Chevalier's plea that he 'could not help himself'.

Secondly, the educated reader was used to meeting 'cruel Fate' and 'fatal passions' in a purely literary context, that of tragedy. Here, since the great bulk of tragedies were set in Classical antiquity, such notions were a proper part of the religious beliefs of the characters. So when the Chevalier throws responsibility for his actions upon *le sort* or *le destin*, we need not suppose that he is being set up as a pagan or a convinced fatalist: these are literary echoes and reminiscences, mere *façons de parler*, but which also serve to strengthen his argument that he has no choice as to his actions.

These verbal associations with tragedy are not only a pseudo-logical weapon of defence for Des Grieux, they also contribute powerfully to the general tone of his discourse. When Montesquieu called the Chevalier and Manon 'un fripon' and 'une catin', he was characterizing them according to their conduct, which he describes as 'basse', judged in cold blood. But the narrative tone of *Manon Lescaut* is not 'low': the Chevalier speaks as an educated man and recalls his feelings with an eloquence which has no vulgarity. That this eloquence carries literary overtones of, and allusions to, the language of tragedy is yet another reason why the reader may be 'taken out of himself' and fail to notice how far Des Grieux is leading him from the cold light of reason and the more cogent moral standards of real life.

Something that has the
appearance of being true or real.

5. Lescaut: Realism and Verisimilitude

At one level, Lescaut might seem to be important almost only for his functional usefulness to the plot of *Manon Lescaut*. Some agent is needed, from the world of gambling and violence, to introduce Des Grieux into the guild of card-sharpers and to provide him with a pistol for his escape from Saint-Lazare. This functional aspect of Lescaut would seem to be reinforced by his sudden arrival on the scene and more especially by his sudden death. In the catastrophe which we feel to be impending, the loss of such a useful practical ally is yet another blow to Des Grieux. (Incidentally, the death of Lescaut means that it falls to M. de T. . . to suggest the ironic vengeance which the Chevalier can take by eating young G. . . M. . .'s supper and sleeping in his bed—a foolhardy proposal touched with vulgarity, and less in keeping with M. de T. . .'s character than with Lescaut's.) It is possible, therefore, to see Lescaut as just another instrument of fate or chance, contributing to the Chevalier's moral downfall to a greater extent than, but in the same way as, the anonymous valet and maid who steal Des Grieux's money.

But Lescaut is more than this. He is also Manon's brother. And since Prévost sets great store on family resemblances, both in character and destiny, Lescaut shares certain traits with Manon herself. In him they are cruder and stronger because he is mature and because these traits are unredeemed by the physical charms and the feminine *douceur* of his sister. It is clear, however, that even if the two have little real affection for each other, there is a profound affinity in their attitudes and outlook. Both are egotistical and devoid of moral scruples. Both are therefore quite prepared to cheat and trick, for their own benefit, richer folk who are fools enough to be gulled. Lescaut is ready to live on his sister's 'earnings' and pimp for her when need arises; and she is equally ready to present herself to the elder G. . . M. . . when Lescaut has paved the way for her. Lacking Manon's charm and beauty, Lescaut seems merely brutish, but they are siblings under the skin.

It is this kinship with Manon which brings him into contact with Des Grieux, for whom he becomes a kind of evil genius. In moments of disaster, when the Chevalier is already downcast and despairing, Lescaut provides both suggestions and practical means for recouping their losses —in ignoble ways. During the crucial central period of Des Grieux's story he makes himself at home in the young couple's Paris lodgings, creating a curious version of a *ménage à trois*, and exerting a kind of domination over the household. The Chevalier finds him repugnant, but he puts up with him for Manon's sake.

After the fire at Chaillot and the disappearance of the casket containing their money, Des Grieux discovers that Lescaut's infamy is far deeper than he had imagined. The barefaced proposal: 'Une fille comme elle devrait nous entretenir, vous, elle et moi' (p. 55) should be enough to make any man of honour turn him out of the house. But the Chevalier realizes that Lescaut is the kind of adviser he needs in this emergency, so he stifles his 'noble' reactions and even pretends to take the suggestion as something of a joke: 'Le besoin que j'avais de lui m'obligea de répondre, en riant, que son conseil était une dernière ressource qu'il fallait remettre à l'extrémité' (p. 56). This *extrémité* arrives, from Lescaut's point of view at least, when the valet and maid decamp with Des Grieux's winnings. Lescaut sees this as the moment to make overtures to M. de G... M.... And in this affair one could argue that he is more considerate and more honest than his sister: he includes Des Grieux in the scheme, in the role of Manon's 'pauvre petit frère orphelin', and he assumes that Manon will give G... M... value for the money and presents received. When Manon decides to trick G... M..., however, the prospect of such a quick profit wins him over.

As card-sharper, trickster, pimp and member of the ill-famed *gardes du corps*, Lescaut comes to represent the shady, trafficking side of Paris life. This is the 'reality' which gradually engulfs and besmirches the Chevalier's dream of an idyllic life with Manon. One way of envisaging *Manon Lescaut* is to consider it as a conflict between the ideal—an innocent natural linking of two young lives in the happiness of love—and the sordid reality of a world in which one must tolerate ignoble people and descend to infamous actions if one is to achieve one's aims. Prévost's picture of 'reality', and the scope of his 'realism' therefore call for some consideration.

Certain kinds of 'realism' have little or no importance in Prévost's fiction. One of these is the importance attributed, by Balzac for instance, to the visible concrete elements of the world. Prévost does not attach any particular significance to *things*: streets, buildings, furniture and clothes. He is, for the most part, not interested in the way they may either influence or express people's personality. Think, for instance, how little we are ever told about the characters' clothes in *Manon Lescaut*. If the dirtiness of Manon's dress is noted by the Man of Quality, it is only in order to point out that this hardly detracted from her appearance. When the young couple set off from Amiens, Manon's luggage consists only of 'son linge', the point being that the Chevalier can easily carry it for her. Des Grieux's first action, on leaving Saint-Sulpice, is to go to a shop where he can change his clerical dress for 'les galons et l'épée'. Clothes for Manon are a matter of practical importance both during and after her escape from the Hôpital. And the fact that the Chevalier is in his night-shirt when M. de G. . . M. . . arrives with two soldiers of the night-watch means that he cannot draw his sword and defend himself and Manon. In every one of these cases the mention of clothing has some direct bearing on the story. Prévost would not dream of describing clothes for their own sake, or helping the reader to visualize the mere panoply of the characters.

Nor does he have any feeling for cities as visual entities with a character of their own, or for the countryside as a subject of poetic or evocative descriptions. He manages to convey Manon and Des Grieux from France to America without even mentioning the sea. And the description he does provide of the landscape which greets them is remarkable by modern standards for its brevity, and by any standards for its negative effect:

> Le pays ne nous offrit rien d'agréable à la première vue. C'étaient des campagnes stériles et inhabitées, où l'on voyait à peine quelques roseaux et quelques arbres dépouillés par le vent. Nulle trace d'hommes ni d'animaux. (p. 184)

Clearly this, like the subsequent brief accounts of the town and of the *misérable cabane* allotted to Manon and Des Grieux, must be intended not so much to help the reader visualize the setting as to suggest the despondency which the new arrivals will inevitably feel upon viewing such a thankless habitat.

The description of physical conditions in North America, and especially the sandy waste in which Manon dies, serve as conclusive proof that Prévost was quite unconcerned about accurate portrayal of real places. As footnotes in modern editions will tell us, the countryside around New Orleans runs to swamp rather than sand. Whether Prévost was ignorant of this, or whether he knew and falsified the facts is, from a literary

point of view, irrelevant. The *désert* was emotively more suited to the
death-scene he wished to portray; and the vast majority of his readers
would know scarcely anything about the 'reality' of the environs of
New Orleans. When the facts are unknown or unsuitable, Prévost
creates a fictitious 'reality' more appropriate to the intended literary
effect. Equally, when a large number of his readers can be expected to
know some specific detail about real life in Paris, Prévost will mention
that detail accurately, because to do otherwise would be foolish. He will
not, however, expand or dilate on such details because his chief concern
is not to build up in the reader's mind an impression of external 'reality'
but to lull the reader into acceptance of the whole story as 'true'. Therefore, although certain references in *Manon Lescaut* can be shown to apply
to real places, such as the Palais-Royal gardens and the Hôtel de Tran-
sylvanie, or to real institutions and practices such as the confinement
of erring young noblemen in Saint-Lazare, these references are made in
the cause of verisimilitude or *vraisemblance* rather than of 'realism' for its
own sake.

During the eighteenth century many writers of memoir-novels and
letter-novels put up a kind of pretence that their works were literally
true, that is, genuine autobiographies or authentic collections of letters.
This pretence was, in part at least, a reaction to various criticisms
frequently levelled at the novel: it was thought to be unsatisfactory on
literary grounds, as an ill-defined genre with no Classical models;
harmful on moral grounds, since it so often gave a spurious attraction to
the disruptive passion of love; and dangerous, again morally, in that it
offered false invented stories as if they were true. Such accusations did not
deter those authors who chose to write fiction, but many novelists did
react, particularly to the allegations of immorality and deceit. To evade
the attack on fiction as 'falsehood', they produced works which were
supposedly based on genuine documents and were therefore not novels
at all.

This was the case for Prévost's *Mémoires et aventures . . .*, which claimed
to be the authentic autobiography of a Man of Quality. As the last volume
of the *Mémoires*, *Manon Lescaut* came under the general guarantee of
being 'true'. Or if one were to consider it, alternatively, as a *nouvelle*,
then again the same standard prevailed, for the *nouvelle* set out to be
'news', a story which had just come to light.

One small detail of Prévost's usage which must have annoyed many
a reader in its time depends entirely on the pretence that this is a true

story about real people: the use of initials instead of full names, as in
M. de B..., M. de G... M..., etc. The convention was that since these
were real people, then they or their relations and friends might be em-
barrassed if they were mentioned by name. The custom is a trivial device
in itself, but its widespread observance throughout the century shows
how firm was the hold of the convention that the novelist was telling
a true story.

The word 'convention' rather than 'pretence' became apt after a time:
on the one hand some successful novelists, unwilling to forego credit
for their work, let it be known that they had invented the 'true' stories;
and on the other, the reading public learned not to take prefatorial
claims of truth too literally. In theory, a writer who convinced his readers
that a given work was wholly true could get away with a sensational
and implausible story, since extraordinary things *do* happen. In practice,
the more skilled authors, and those who had doubts about how far they
could deceive the public over 'truth', took steps to make their fictions
credible and convincing. Thus in *Manon Lescaut* we can find some elements where Prévost has shown a certain respect for the canons of
verisimilitude, together with others where literary conventions replace
or even flout *vraisemblance*.

Let us consider, for instance, those elements of the novel which involve
speech and dialogue. At the very basis of the narrative situation there is an
assumption which is surely quite implausible: that the Man of Quality
can listen to Des Grieux talking for several hours and then write down,
almost immediately, a full and entirely accurate account of what he said.
Here Prévost is simply following a long-accepted convention, the myth
of the listener who has, in modern terms, a tape-recorder memory. This
falls at the opposite end of the scale of verisimilitude from the use of
initials to avoid giving 'real' names; but most readers do not query it
because the device is so familiar that it is ignored.

Des Grieux's story need not come into the same category of im-
plausibility concerning the narration, since he is looking back over his
own life. But the criteria of verisimilitude can still provoke some queries:
does what we read suggest a man talking? Do his powers of memory
seem exaggerated when, for instance, he reports conversations? And
does he convey the remarks of others in a convincing way?

The Chevalier's style does not in any simple straightforward manner
suggest a spoken narrative, if only because it is devoid of the weaknesses
that characterize the speech of all but the most accomplished talkers:

no hesitations, stumblings, clumsy repetitions or self-corrections. On the other hand, it reads well aloud, falling for the most part into the easy rhythms of speech rather than the elaborate sentence-convolutions of a Henry James or a Proust. The opening pages are noticeably effective from this point of view. They illustrate one of the factors which contribute to the easy effect of the Chevalier's style: the sentences are nearly all of the simple Subject + Verb construction. Only rarely do we find an initial clause postponing the main verb, and even then there is little to hold up the reader: 'Quoiqu'elle fût encore moins âgée que moi, elle reçut mes politesses sans paraître embarrassée' (pp. 19–20). Prévost is quite capable of formulating long and complex sentences, in for instance his articles in *Le Pour et Contre*. It would therefore seem that he deliberately controlled the naturalistic flow of the Chevalier's style.

We can hear the words of others only through Des Grieux's version of their talk. Does he, like the Man of Quality, appear to have more-than-human powers of memory, or has Prévost kept the conversations within the bounds of plausibility? Here we find a nice blend of the implausible and of literary skill. Analysis of the Chevalier's narrative shows that about half of it is devoted to exchanges between the characters. It is hardly likely that anyone could recall so much talk in detail, especially as some of the conversations go back several years. Prévost has glossed over this difficulty by a technique which conceals how much Des Grieux is supposed to remember. He alternates the occasional remark in direct speech with longer passages of reported speech which often suggest that he is conveying the gist of the talk rather than the actual words. This device has two advantages. We scarcely realize how much of Des Grieux's story consists of conversations which he could hardly have recalled in faithful detail. And the sentences quoted in direct speech acquire an emphasis which they would not receive if the whole conversation were to be set out in the kind of dialogue used by omniscient narrators like Balzac and Flaubert. The Chevalier can use this aspect of the technique to his own advantage on occasion. For instance, in the discussion with Tiberge about happiness, Des Grieux puts his own point of view at length, in direct speech, while Tiberge's arguments are given more briefly, in reported speech, except for a condemnation of Des Grieux's comparisons and for the much-quoted (because so striking in its effect): 'Dieu me pardonne, je pense que voici encore un de nos ansénistes' (p. 93).

A new problem concerning verisimilitude arises when we consider the

remarks in direct speech attributed to other characters, since every-
thing in the story comes to us *via* the Chevalier. One might suppose, for
instance, that an accurate rendering of Lescaut's speech-habits would
include a number of military oaths, and that the angry cab-driver would
launch into vituperation when deprived of his promised tip. Since
Des Grieux is a gentleman, however, and well-educated, and since he has
Renoncour and Rosemont as his audience, it is not *vraisemblable* that
he should descend to such vulgar forms of speech. A certain unity of
tone imposed on the dialogue of other characters, and a lessening of their
vulgarity in purely verbal terms is therefore nearer to the 'truth' of how
Des Grieux told the story. Nevertheless Prévost does manage, by
sentence-structure as well as by the meaning conveyed, to make some
differentiation between the various levels of education and class among
the characters. In reply to Des Grieux's dramatic—or melodramatic—
'Il faut défendre ta vie ou me faire retrouver Manon', Lescaut retorts
flatly: 'Là! que vous êtes vif!' (p. 70). His language is, in general, practical
and down-to-earth; and of course his plans are base and predatory. By
contrast, the good-hearted Marcel, whose account of Manon is only
reported, is given a simple familiar style: 'Il nous dit que c'était une
douceur angélique; qu'il n'avait jamais reçu d'elle un mot de dureté . . .'
(p. 102). Prévost does not attempt here to make the Chevalier indicate
any kind of lower-class accent, as might be appropriate for Marcel.
This particular kind of realistic or naturalistic effect was at the time
usually found only in comic and burlesque works. Similarly we are
left to imagine for ourselves, with no indications in the text to help us,
what kind of an accent Des Grieux himself assumed, to go with his 'air
simple et provincial', when he acted the part of Manon's little brother
and made naïve remarks to M. de G. . . M. . . . .

   This little scene of disguise and *double entendre* raises the question of
another and quite different form of realism or *vraisemblance* in *Manon*:
the inclusion of comic elements. It can be said that Classical French
tragedy is unrealistic, or not true to the whole of life, in its insistence on
the elevated, serious and emotional aspects of human conduct. The whole
truth about anyone's life will include ridiculous as well as noble details.
In spite of the generally tragic aura with which Prévost invests *Manon*,
he also manages to bring in touches of comedy; besides the play-acting
for the benefit of M. de G. . . M. . . , there is, for instance, the occasion
when Des Grieux endangers the escape-plan by forgetting to bring a
pair of breeches for Manon's disguise. Yet laughable as this little lapse

undoubtedly is, it is conveyed discreetly, and not allowed to create too violent a contrast to the prevailing tone.

The question of the tone of the Chevalier's discourse brings us to the subject of Prévost's revisions and corrections. For the edition of 1753 he went carefully through the text and made, in all, some six hundred changes. The most important was the insertion of a whole new episode, to be discussed in the next chapter. Of the alterations to the existing text, many were small grammatical touches, such as the substitution of *pas* for *point*. Other emendations removed awkward turns of phrase, improved the flow of one sentence, made the sense of another more clear. The novel had by now proved its popularity, and Prévost evidently thought it worth while spending some time polishing a work which had probably been written in haste.

Apart from the stylistic corrections, Prévost made a number of changes to the vocabulary, all of which tended to make the narrative sound more noble and refined. These changes occur in Renoncour's introduction as well as in Des Grieux's own narrative: 'un mauvais cabaret' is turned into 'une mauvaise hôtellerie' (p. 10), etc. The general effect is to diminish or eliminate some of the elements which might be called 'realistic'—in the sense of suggesting the more vulgar, less refined aspects of life. Some modern readers may regret this edulcoration, though its effects are slight. But we cannot accuse Prévost of making the work as a whole less plausible. He has merely made the narrators consistently more careful and refined in their choice of terms. The Chevalier's narrative in particular is a complex and subtle vehicle which achieves a variety of functions: it portrays the Chevalier's character, class and beliefs both explicitly and by implication; it conveys the characters of others, with slight but significant variations in reported speech which suggest *their* personality and station in life; it relates various actions and events ranging from childish gaiety to the macabre final catastrophe, its discussions move between the humdrum practical details of daily life and rarefied concepts like divine grace; and all this with sufficient consistency of tone and manner for us to believe that a single narrator could feel and talk in this way. It is one of the paradoxes of the work that all these multiple inter-related processes are expressed in a style which seems clear, straightforward and simple. This apparent simplicity, which in fact conceals a wealth of artistic skill, is undoubtedly one of the elements in the novel's continuing appeal.

6. Manon's 'Protectors': The Role of Money

Having discussed Prévost's treatment of, so to speak, the visible and audible world of *Manon Lescaut*, we can turn now to the workings of society as seen in the book, and in particular to the role of money. Since this is one of the major factors in the plot, we shall also consider how Prévost structures and motivates the successive stages of the plot.

Of all the characters in the book who have a decisive role in the action, the three who are least defined as individuals and therefore the least memorable must surely be the men who pay for Manon's favours: M. de B..., M. de G...M..., and the younger G...M.... (It seems unfortunate that they, of all people, should lack the full names which might help us to distinguish and remember them.) Their lack of definition is understandable on several counts: Prévost does not let Des Grieux meet them often enough, or long enough, to learn to know them; the Chevalier does not want to know them, since they are threats to his continuing life with Manon; and finally, these men are more important as types than as individuals—they are Wealth, and any rich man could have won Manon when they did.

The conflict between the Chevalier's ideal life and reality has already been mentioned. One major element in this conflict is money. The ideas of a young man like Des Grieux would have three sources: the aristo-cratic values of his family, and the classical and religious books he had studied. None of these would prepare him for a situation in which mere money could dictate his way of life; such sordid considerations could not occupy the mind of a gentleman or a scholar. His dream of life with Manon puts their existence on the level of a Princesse de Clèves or a Phèdre, in which it is the emotions which matter, and practical details do not impinge on the lovers. Manon's ideas, in accordance with her humble birth, are less elevated. She seems to set little store on the stability and permanence which the Chevalier longs for; she cannot be happy with an existence filled only by love—and her diversions must be paid for.

We are so used to the importance of money in modern fiction that it may be difficult to grasp how startling the irruption of this element into serious love-stories must have seemed to readers of the early eighteenth century. (Once again one must distinguish between serious stories and the comic or picaresque type of fiction.) Prévost was not the first to incorporate in his writings this new element of realism. Many of the *nouvelles* which dealt with the recent past had already used this factor in varying ways. In one of Challes's stories, for instance, the crisis comes when the virtuous Angélique, expensively dressed, is seen by a noble-woman whom she respects, and who assumes that such lavish attire must indicate that Angélique has sold her virtue. Once Angélique can explain that she came by her money and her finery in an honourable way, the story speeds on to a happy ending. In *Manon Lescaut*, Prévost has so organized his plot that practically all the major events depend, in one way or another, upon money.

We need not go into tedious detail to demonstrate this fact, since it is obvious enough. But one element which does perhaps require comment is the combination of chance and of psychological motivation in the actions involving money.

When the young people run away from Amiens they have a sum worth, by present standards, something over £100. At this stage neither of them has any notion of the problems of lack of money, and Prévost underlines their childish lack of foresight: 'Nous nous imaginâmes, comme des enfants sans expérience, que cette somme ne finirait jamais' (p. 22). By the time that Des Grieux begins to realize that their resources may run out, and suggests an appeal to his father, Manon, in her more practical way, has already seen the need for a further source of income. She raises objections to Des Grieux's plan, but in such a way that he comments: 'Je n'eus pas le moindre soupçon du coup cruel qu'on se préparait à me porter' (p. 26). (Notice incidentally how the use of *on* rather than *elle* transfers the blame away from Manon.) This 'cruel blow' depends on two factors: Manon's willingness to sell her favours, and the unhappy chance that they had taken rooms in the street where M. de B. . . lived and could thus catch sight of Manon.

In the two main incidents which follow the renewal of the love-affair, after Saint-Sulpice, Prévost again uses external agencies, which have an air of pure chance, to deprive the couple of their money. Again it so 'happens' that the lodgings they take in Paris are in the same street as Lescaut's, and he battens on them, getting them to pay his debts and entertain his friends. To aggravate this situation comes the fire in their Chaillot house in which the casket containing their capital disappears.

Obviously one could create a subsidiary story about how the fire started and who carried off the casket, but Prévost does not here attempt any such explanation, preferring to portray the event as 'un funeste accident' (p. 52). On the next occasion he does set out more explicitly, and with swift economical detail, the human background to the vanishing of their money and clothes: the valet and maid, in love, who hear Manon and Des Grieux planning to invest his winnings, and who make off with this wealth in their employers' absence. But again the general effect is of a bolt from the blue, another 'accident'. Chance is thus hostile to the lovers. Admittedly, good luck seems for a time to be on the side of the Chevalier, since he can win so much at cards—but only because he cheats. Chance, it seems, is always waiting to deprive the lovers of the money they have acquired, by various dubious means. Viewed in the perspective of conventional morality, chance is thus working on the side of justice; but from Des Grieux's point of view such 'accidents' are cruel blows to his dream of a life of innocent love.

Equally cruel, if more easily explained in human terms, are the disasters brought upon the lovers by the elder G. . . M. . . . He is motivated largely by the fact that they have tricked him out of money. (Additional motives are that he has been made to look a fool and that, in the second incident, he is moved by fear for his son's welfare.) And he brings into play, in contrast to the random effects of chance, all the complicated punitive machinery of organized society—the reformatory, prison, deportation. Society did not interfere while the lovers were merely 'living in sin', but when they took to crime, and crimes involving money, the forces of order reacted. It is not without significance, in relation to the ethical standards implicit in the story, that Des Grieux's murder of the porter at Saint-Lazare is hushed up and goes unpunished. Society is more concerned with offences against the purse than the person.

Money is thus used, in a variety of ways, as the immediate occasion for much of the action in the plot; it is lost by chance, and gained by crime—which leads to punishment. But such a description might apply to a modern crime novel or a drama of conspiracy on the Stock Exchange. In *Manon*, money is not an end in itself, it is needed by Des Grieux only to keep Manon happy, and therefore faithful.

Prévost introduced, when he revised the work in 1753, an episode which altered the simple recurring pattern of the work as he had first written it. The incident involving the Italian prince (pp. 118–24) shows us a Manon who, for the first time in the novel, rejects the offers of a

rich man. The effect of this may be, in part, to prepare us for the con-
verted and constant Manon of New Orleans. The episode underlines
the fact we have already noted, that Manon does not desire money for
its own sake; as long as the Chevalier can provide for parties of pleasure,
she prefers life with him to a possibly more luxurious existence with
anyone else. And the incident is preceded by a passage summing up their
current assets. Their capital is small enough, a mere hundred pistoles
borrowed from the long-suffering Tiberge, but the Chevalier has proved
that he can make a more than adequate income by card-sharping, and
what is more, he has prospects in the form of a legacy from his mother
which he is now old enough to claim (p. 117). He is confident and cheer-
ful about the future. Thus when the Italian offers her, 'au delà des monts,
une brillante fortune et des adorations éternelles', she can resist the apparent temptation. We should also remember that Manon *is* fond of the
Chevalier, in her fashion. Her first betrayal of him was motivated, or so
at least she claims, by a desire to get money so that they could continue
living together. When she heard of his return to Paris it was she who, of
her own accord, sought him out. And her plans for life with M. de G. . .
M. . . included Des Grieux. But she could hardly suppose that the Italian
prince would transport the Chevalier 'au delà des monts', so the offer
implies separation from Des Grieux as well as wealth. It is quite in keeping with her attitudes and actions so far that she should reject the proposal. Her doing so emphasizes that insofar as she is capable of love at
that point, she does love Des Grieux. And the manner of her doing it
simultaneously illustrates the playful and the childishly cruel sides of her
character. The episode also enriches the story as a whole by giving us an
impression of one of the peaceful and happy periods of the love-affair.

   Critics vary in their response to this added episode. It has one clear
disadvantage, that of throwing Prévost's chronology out of gear. When
Des Grieux's father arrives in Paris, it is in response to the letter written
'huit jours auparavant' (p. 159). But the interval since the sending of the
letter has been extended by the several weeks which allow for the new
episode. Another objection is that the episode is too light-hearted in
tone, and therefore does not fit into the mood of impending tragedy.
Counter-objections can be raised: it seems unlikely, for instance, that
most readers would notice, without the pedantic reminder of a footnote, the discrepancy of chronology; and the gaiety of the incident may
be said to heighten, by its contrast, the ensuing catastrophe. Criticisms
on either side depend on the knowledge that Prévost had introduced this

new element when revising the text. I suspect that if we lacked this piece of knowledge, we might take the episode for granted (as Prévost doubtless wished his readers to do) as an integral part of the story. Good or bad, an ill-judged interpolation or an enrichment of the original, this episode certainly introduces a new note into the pattern. The would-be 'protector' is rejected, anxiety about money fades into the background, the Chevalier's jealous fears are shown to be groundless, and the disasters ahead are put off, for a while, by 'l'humeur folâtre de Manon'.

7. Des Grieux père and Tiberge: Two Moral Codes

At the point in his life when he begins his story, the Chevalier has the support and affection of two people, his father and Tiberge. These two men continue, throughout his adventures, to love him and to act, according to their lights, on his behalf. If one sees the story in terms of a conflict between Good and Evil, then just as Manon is the eternal temptress and Lescaut is the Chevalier's evil angel, so Tiberge is his guardian angel and Des Grieux *père* is the Father who condemns and punishes his son's fall from grace.

The parallel should not be taken too far: even if the Chevalier's father is on the side of Good, his ethical code is based not so much on religion as on the secular ideals of the *honnête homme*. In this system the supreme value is honour, rather than the Christian ideal of virtue. We discover the father's ideas at an early stage, when Des Grieux is brought back from his first stay in Paris. There are 'quelques reproches généraux' for the Chevalier's disobedience in running away without his father's leave. As for Des Grieux's relations with Manon, his father takes a tolerant view: this affair will teach the boy to be more careful. He refers to it as 'cette petite aventure', a mere *peccadillo*. He is certainly not concerned with the notion of sin; there is no solemn warning on the evils of sexual licence and fornication. In fact Des Grieux *père* finds his son's naïvety about Manon highly amusing—one must be credulous indeed to expect 'love' and 'constancy' from such a girl.

However, when it becomes clear that Des Grieux's feelings are deeply involved, his father abandons such teasing and discusses the affair seriously, putting forward reasons which might help, in the Chevalier's words, to 'me ramener au bon sens et m'inspirer du mépris pour l'infidèle Manon'. Again there is no appeal to religion: it is mere 'good sense' to accept that the affair is over, and as a nobleman Des Grieux should feel only contempt for someone who can so easily break faith.

The Chevalier's father has a strong sense of rank and of the duties and privileges that go with it. His first reproach to Des Grieux, when he

visits him in prison, is that he has become a by-word and thus, by implication, brought dishonour on the family name. And he goes on to contrast
the *honnête homme* which Des Grieux's upbringing had prepared him to
be with the *fripon* he has turned into: 'un fils vicieux qui a perdu tous
sentiments d'honneur' (p. 162). The Chevalier defends himself in the
same kind of terms. He has not abandoned honour and duty, even though
love has forced him into some discreditable actions; and many gentle-
men of good birth have committed the same offences. But, he concludes,
'il me restait trop d'honneur pour ne pas me condamner moi-même'
(p. 164).

From all this it is clear that Des Grieux both understands his father's
code of ethics and accepts it. On this subject at least they talk the same
language. The Chevalier refers more than once, regretfully, to the fact
that some of his actions are dishonourable. However, the strange
distortion which even the concept of honour can undergo through the
workings of love is illustrated by his remark on learning that Manon
agrees simply to take G. . . M. . . 's money and then run off:

> Sa résolution me fut beaucoup plus agréable que l'espérance des cinq
> mille livres. J'eus lieu de reconnaître que mon cœur n'avait point
> encore perdu tout sentiment d'honneur, puisqu'il était si satisfait
> d'échapper à l'infamie. (p. 75)

The 'infamy' was his pretence of being Manon's brother and living on
G. . . M. . . 's money. Since this ignoble plan has been abandoned, his
'honour' is preserved—though he is going to live on the sum Manon has
inveigled out of the old man. Honesty and plain dealing are not covered
by the Chevalier's notion of honour.

It is, however, this code which triumphs when Manon is dead. Once
the temptations and stresses of love are over, the Chevalier can return
to the values of his younger, more innocent days:

> Mais le Ciel . . . avait dessein de me rendre utiles mes malheurs et ses
> châtiments. Il m'éclaira de ses lumières, qui me firent rappeler des
> idées dignes de ma naissance et de mon éducation. . . . Je me livrai
> entièrement aux inspirations de l'honneur. (p. 202)

This passage, as we now read it in the 1753 version, contains some changes
from the original text. There, Des Grieux was touched by 'les lumières
de la grâce', experienced true repentance, and devoted himself not to
honour but 'aux exercices de la piété'. A religious conversion has been

replaced by a return to the ideals of the nobleman and the *honnête homme*. In the Deloffre-Picard edition, a footnote points out the merits of the change in terms of characterization and credibility. The religious life, exemplified by Des Grieux's stay at Saint-Sulpice, did not appear to affect him profoundly, since he could give it up with so little hesitation. A second religious conversion might therefore carry little assurance of his ability to remain in the path of virtue. The values of his class and family, more deeply ingrained, are likely to be a more reliable guide. This comment is a sound one. Above all, the Chevalier who is now relat-ing his adventures does not give us, his readers, the impression of a man in whom religious principles and repentance have triumphed.. Apart from other indications, the word *péché* is not in his vocabulary. He admits to a career involving *désordres* and *faiblésses* and *égarements*, but we do not hear him confess, in all humility, 'Peccavi'.

One might argue that Prévost's alteration of the text at this point produces a confusion of thought. The code of *honnêteté* does not rely on the intervention of Heaven to enforce its values; dishonour, shame, loss of *gloire*, are punishments inflicted by society. Indeed, since Christian virtues include humility, the concept of honour itself may come into conflict with religious values. If this were the only occasion in the narra-tive where Des Grieux's ethical arguments were confused, then Prévost's emendations could well be blamed. However, the Chevalier is consist-ently strong on feeling but weak in analytical thought, and on several occasions he has already shown a tendency to try and combine the secular ethics of *honnêteté* with the Christian moral code—not to mention his references to a kind of fatalism.

Consider for instance the blending of notions from different fields of reference in the paragraph beginning: 'Je sentis tout le prix de sa généro-sité' (p. 61). The 'générosité' refers to Tiberge's loan, and Des Grieux might well be grateful, considering that Tiberge has pledged his future salary so as to help the couple. This gratitude is so intense that it even enables him to see his love as something regrettable. But the passion is ineluctable and irresistible, 'l'aveuglement d'un amour fatal qui me faisait violer tous les devoirs'. At this point his views are not those of an orthodox Christian, who would not admit the Chevalier's plea of help-lessness in the face of love. The next sentence elaborates what went before: his impulse of regret was a good one, and becomes 'la vertu', which momentarily conflicts with love. 'La vertu', combined with the term 'lumière', takes us into the domain of Christian concepts; by the light of grace, virtue is again active in the Chevalier's heart. But what this light reveals is 'la honte et l'indignité de mes chaînes'. This phrase-ology suggest wounded honour rather than vice or sin. In religious terms, Des Grieux's behaviour is an offence against God— for whom he has substituted Manon—and also to the Church and its sacraments, since he is living with Manon outside the bonds of wedlock. Shame and humiliation are thus not adequate reactions for a Christian.

'Mais ce combat fut léger et dura peu.' Since he has already qualified his love as *fatal*, we can expect it to triumph over vague impulses to-wards virtue. He then elaborates on the strength of his feeling for Manon, and reproaches himself for his fleeting inclination to characterize as shameful 'une tendresse si juste pour un objet si charmant'. The delight-fully balanced cadence goes with a complex summing-up of his position. His affection is just, right and proper (not shameful), and what justifies it is Manon's 'charm', the spell she has cast over him, her fascination. This restores him to the role of a helpless victim.

If this were meant as a piece of reasoned argument, we could be scornful. But it is of course a different exercise altogether, an emotional justification which shows the kinds of 'reasons' such a young man would deploy to quell his scruples.

This brief moral combat arises after one of Des Grieux's meetings with Tiberge, who is the representative of religious values in the novel. In much fiction of the period, it is the hero's mother who voices the Christian ethic, but one can see a number of reasons why Prévost chose a young cleric to do this instead. At the practical level, he can meet Des Grieux, lend him money, and follow him to America, activities which a mother could not easily engage in. And the spectacle of Des Grieux's mother trying to wrest her son from Manon's charms would introduce psychological complications unsuited to the clear line of Prévost's plot. It therefore falls to Tiberge to act as a counterbalance to the secular morality expressed by the Chevalier's father.

Tiberge also provides a counterpart to the love-affair itself, for there is a marked similarity between his attitude towards Des Grieux and Des Grieux's attitude towards Manon. However badly Manon behaves, the Chevalier's affection is never weakened; and Tiberge shows the same willingness to overlook Des Grieux's lapses. Whatever Manon requires to be happy, the Chevalier will try to obtain for her; and Tiberge does as much for him. Manon's wishes or needs arise from principles quite different from Des Grieux's own, but he understands them and explains them without condemnation; Tiberge cannot accept Des Grieux's philosophy of love, but he too shows a sympathetic understanding. And as a final, more practical touch, just as the Chevalier is willing to give up his familiar life and go to the New World with Manon, so Tiberge makes the hazardous journey to America in order to help Des Grieux. He is clearly a paragon among friends. The continuing devotion of this selfless and virtuous man must help to suggest, as the novel progresses, that the Chevalier is a person worthy of sympathy and affection.

We do not really need to analyse closely what Tiberge says. In the main, his arguments are those which any convinced Christian might put forward. But one may properly ask whether his affection and his willingness to forgive Des Grieux's errors do not sometimes lead him into excessive toleration, amounting to support, for such weakness. The clearest instance of this is the occasion when Des Grieux appeals to him for money after the fire at Chaillot. Tiberge, after some inner debate, agrees to provide what is wanted, in the hope that once Des Grieux's mind is easy on the score of money, he will revert to 'la sagesse et la vérité (p. 60). The reasoning is specious and does more credit to Tiberge's kindness than to the clarity of his principles.

Elsewhere Tiberge voices the claims of religion with more coherent arguments. If he does not carry the day, it is of course largely because the Chevalier's mind is not open to rational persuasion. His tactics with Tiberge are either to simulate agreement, by suppressing some part of the truth, or else to argue back, but from the standpoint of quite different premisses.

The various deceptions which Des Grieux practises upon Tiberge must surely be classed—when we are considering the matter in cold blood—as among his most ignoble actions. Here he is trading upon friendship rather than cheating strangers who have no particular claim upon him. The process begins within minutes of Des Grieux's first meeting with Manon, when he conceals from Tiberge their plan to run away the very next morning. In the same way he later suppresses, in conversation with Tiberge, the fact that he has helped Manon escape from the Hôpital and that they are living together again.

On these occasions Tiberge is reassured, though without good cause, as to the Chevalier's intentions. He is less happy after those conversations where Des Grieux defends his love. Here the Chevalier as narrator influences our impressions of the debate, for his own side of the discussion is given more prominence than Tiberge's point of view. But in any case the latter's efforts are doomed to failure, for Des Grieux does not accept the basic concepts from which Tiberge starts. In the case of the secular code of *honnêteté* Des Grieux, as we have seen, does continue to meet his father on common ground. With Tiberge the case is altered. In their long and important discussion about the nature of happiness (pp. 90–3), Tiberge and Des Grieux can never have any meeting of minds since their basic assumptions are totally opposed. The Chevalier defends the merits of earthly physical happiness as compared with the felicity of the immortal soul—a position no Christian would entertain. The attractions of happiness here-and-now are so obvious and perceptible that they are worth paying for by some suffering, and it is only to be expected that they should win more converts than the remote satisfactions of a religion which requires 'une pratique triste et mortifiante'. But he has admitted the notion that the felicity of the soul in Heaven will surpass earthly happiness, and this gives Tiberge an opening to ask why he does not prefer and pursue this greater happiness. Des Grieux's answer, that he lacks the strength to give up Manon, and Tiberge's scandalized rejoinder that such an argument smacks of Jansenism, have given rise in the past to much critical discussion on the religious implications of Des Grieux's views.[1]

One can of course consider his reactions purely in terms of orthodox Christian concepts. This is how the Man of Quality presents the case in the *Avis de l'Auteur*: Des Grieux 'refuses' happiness, he presses forward 'volontairement' towards ruin and disaster—with the implication that had he so chosen, he could have behaved otherwise. Within this schema, Des Grieux's plea that he cannot give up Manon does indeed suggest the unorthodox or Jansenist notion that a given individual may yield to sin because God has not granted him the grace to resist temptation. But it is the Man of Quality, and later on Tiberge, who select this framework of ideas. As we have seen, the Chevalier himself tends for the most part to account for his inability to resist by referring either to his inherent sensibility or else to the active directing force of Fate, which is envisaged in a quasi-pagan manner. Since these notions are quite outside the scope of Tiberge's faith, the two men's point of view can never coincide and permit real argument.

At the end of the story, however, Tiberge sees the success of his efforts.

[1] Cf. especially Paul Hazard, *Études critiques sur 'Manon Lescaut'* (University of Chicago Press, 1929), pp. 47–69.

Arriving in New Orleans, he learns that Des Grieux has returned to virtue. We may be somewhat less than convinced by this change of heart. However, the subject of Des Grieux's conversion and that of Manon calls for separate consideration, together with the significance of the voyage to the New World.

8. The New World: The Dénouement and the Moral

Manon, as we have already noticed, has come to be accepted and cited as an archetypal figure. In such mentions, the reference is always to the gay, pleasure-loving girl of the first nine-tenths of the novel; her conversion is neglected or ignored. Similarly, Des Grieux is remembered as the victim of passion rather than as the sadder but wiser young man who returns from America. This rejection or neglect of the dénouement is comprehensible, for in America both Manon and Des Grieux turn to conventional modes of thinking, and thus seem to relinquish some of the exceptional qualities which have captured so many readers' imagination. We need therefore to give some special consideration to this last episode and the kind of changes in character which it involves.

Critics vary in their views on how far Manon's 'conversion' is likely or plausible. I feel that quite a good case can be put up for it. In religious terms one could say that she has been purified by suffering and has now come to understand the meaning of moral values. In the language of modern psychology, her new outlook is the consequence of a traumatic experience—the shame and fear connected with deportation—and of her accession to emotional maturity. Des Grieux's own explanation relies on the concepts of 'essentialist' psychology. Manon at last has the opportunity to fulfil her innate potentialities for virtue: 'Elle était droite et naturelle dans tous ses sentiments, qualité qui dispose toujours à la vertu' (p. 190). Des Grieux too is 'naturally' good; it is the changed circumstances which allow him to follow his essential inclinations.[1]

Prévost thus chooses to close his story with a Manon redeemed, a repentant Magdalen. The New World, belying all Des Grieux's fears, would appear to have allowed the fulfilment of his dream. In this other Eden, his idyll is realized.

However, Prévost did not see fit, as a moral or an aesthetic conclusion, to let the lovers settle down and live happily ever after. The factors which lead up to the ultimate disaster include the new ideas of the couple,

[1] Cf. p. 25 above, and *Manon Lescaut*, Introduction, pp. cx-cxi.

and their consequent desire to get married. But equally important are certain elements which repeatedly influenced their actions in France. Thus, Manon still exerts her fatal charm, and Synnelet is touched by her beauty 'dès le jour de [son] arrivée' (p. 192). And as always, Des Grieux reacts with fury to the idea of anyone else possessing Manon, and will fight for her to the death. Prévost has thus maintained, even after the protagonists' moral revolution, those conditions which we have seen to be crucial factors in all the adventures in France. And despite the New World's apparent promise of a fresh start, Manon's beauty and the Chevalier's passion will lead, here as in Europe, to downfall and disaster.

In spite of the tragic tone in which Des Grieux relates 'un malheur qui n'eut jamais d'exemple', the simple facts of the case include elements of the grotesque. When Synnelet, in the duel, falls at the Chevalier's feet 'sans mouvement', the Chevalier assumes that he is dead. It is on this assumption that he and Manon run away from New Orleans. But the assumption was unjustified. Manon's death is a consequence of the fact that Des Grieux did not bend down and see whether Synnelet's heart was still beating. This is the cold, commonsense interpretation of the facts. But the Chevalier's presentation of them creates a different and a much more moving and poetic sequence of events. It is the crowning example of Prévost's skill in concealing a banal, prosaic view of the world behind a more noble and touching version of 'the truth'.

Des Grieux lays the responsibility for Manon's death on Heaven itself. We have noted how often he mentioned Fate or the stars as the forces which controlled the main events of his life. When it comes to more specific actions, which can hardly be blamed upon such sources, he usually shifts the responsibility on to other people. Many a reader must have been surprised or shocked by Des Grieux's accusing question to Lescaut, after having killed the porter with a shot from his pistol: 'C'est votre faute, pourquoi me l'apportiez vous chargé?' (p. 97). In this and similar situations Des Grieux, who is not above using Christian casuistry when it suits his book, resorts to the theory of intentions: one is guilty of a sin or crime only if one had that end in view. Since he did not intend to kill the porter, he cannot be guilty of murder. In the final catastrophe no other human can be blamed, and Des Grieux considers that Heaven must be responsible. The disaster has struck him like a punishment for crime, although, he protests once again, the punishment is undeserved since he is now prepared to sanctify his love-affair by marrying Manon.

Virtuous or not, he escapes from New Orleans with Manon, and endures the anguish of seeing her die. The love-song has come to its end.

Our final sight of Des Grieux will again vary, depending on whether we take a cold analytical view of the facts or accept the impression he seeks to create. In the former case, the future does not look too bleak for him: he is physically well, legally safe, financially secure and morally regenerated. His grief for Manon's death must be balanced by the memory of the love she finally proved to him, and by his resolve to redeem the family name. If, on the other hand, we rely on the effect of the Chevalier's own narrative, this too leaves some room for comfort. To the grief he feels for Manon is added a sense of guilt over his father's death, but he has regained a certain tranquillity of mind, and can recount the events of his life with a degree of composure, if not with detachment.

But if he emerges from the ordeal in this fashion, what has become of the 'exemple terrible' which was promised us in the *Avis de l'auteur*? Perhaps we should look for the cautionary lesson not in the Chevalier's final situation but in his sufferings during the love-affair? But he says repeatedly that the happiness of living with Manon was so great as to justify and make up for all his sufferings. Once, at the very beginning of his story, he expresses the wish that he had never met Manon, but this wish is belied by the fervour of all the remaining narrative. Quite clearly, the Chevalier accepts that ' 'Tis better to have loved and lost. . .'. With his notions on the nobility of the *âme sensible*, a life without some such experience of passion would be empty indeed.

It is easy to discuss the matter as though the Chevalier were a real person with ideas of his own, which contradict those of the Man of Quality. But of course it is two separate and contrasting pronouncements by Prévost that we must attempt to reconcile or explain. My own view is that the Prévost of the *Avis* is trying—as he often did in real life, and as he makes Des Grieux do also—to absolve himself of responsibility for what is blameworthy by assuring us of his good intentions: You may think that this is an immoral story, but I meant it as a cautionary tale. We can accept such a plea without having to decide whether the protest is entirely honest, whether Prévost was deceiving himself or whether it was a deliberate attempt to deceive the reader. As for the story itself, Prévost may equally well have meant us to see the weakness of the Chevalier's self-defence and take a lesson in self-knowledge from his specious pleas. But as we have the whole novel to measure against Prévost's possible intentions, we have a right to pronounce on his success or failure. The verdict seems to me plain enough: those readers who find the Chevalier too weak or too emotional to hold their interest will not benefit from his adventures; while readers who can accept, in imagination, the Chevalier's point of view will see the glories and perils of love as one of the richest of human experiences, to be sought after rather than avoided. Under Prévost's pen, the fascination of Manon and the willing servitude of Des Grieux transgress and transcend morality.

The passing of the Ancien Régime and the decline of the mode of *sensibilité* have made *Manon Lescaut* in some respects a period piece. Some of the vibrant immediacy of its appeal is doubtless lost to the twentieth-century reader. (And considering its moral import, this may be just as well.) Whether it will continue to attract readers in decades and centuries to come, as social changes make our world even more different from that of Des Grieux, one can hardly say. But its merits are still potent enough, if we give Prévost his head, to carry us into that room in the Lion d'Or, where a pale young man, confident that even in blaming him we will pity him too, begins his story: 'J'avais dix-sept ans. . .'.

Bibliographical Note

Of the many available editions of *Manon Lescaut*, the most useful is the one prepared by Frédéric Deloffre and Raymond Picard (Paris, Garnier, 1965). It contains a long and extremely thorough Introduction, the text of the revised 1753 edition, all the important variants from the other eighteenth-century editions, and a good bibliography of works relating to *Manon*. A short general study on Prévost, with a substantial section on *Manon*, is Henri Roddier's *L'Abbé Prévost, l'homme et l'oeuvre* (Paris, Hatier-Bovin, 1955, in the series *Connaissance des Lettres*). For a more detailed study of Prévost students should consult Jean Sgard, *Prévost romancier* (Paris, Corti, 1968). Also well worth consulting is the collection of papers in *L'Abbé Prévost, Actes du Colloque d'Aix-en-Provence* (Aix-en-Provence, Editions Ophyrs, 1965). Two general works on the background to eighteenth-century French fiction are: Vivienne Mylne, *The Eighteenth Century French Novel* (Manchester, 1965) and the interesting study by Georges May, *Le Dilemme du roman au XVIIIe siècle* (Paris, Presses universitaires, 1963).